MEMORIES
OF THE
LIVING DEAD

COMPILED BY
BOB MICHELUCCI

Copyright © 2013, 2018 by Robert V. Michelucci
Published by Robert V. Michelucci, Pittsburgh, PA
All Rights Reserved.

Cover illustration courtesy: Questar Magazine
Cover image character: © Image Ten, Inc. and used with permission from Kyra Schon
Electronic text illustrations by Robert V. Michelucci
Interior book design & additional editing by Robert J. Michelucci

No part of this publication may be used or reproduced, stored or entered into a retrieval system, transmitted, photocopied, recorded, or otherwise reproduced in any form by any mechanical or electronic means, without prior written permission of the author, expect for brief quotations used in articles and reviews.

First edition: 2013
Revised edition: 2018
ISBN-13: 978-0615845012 (Robert V. Michelucci)
ISBN-10: 0615845010

ACKNOWLEDGEMENTS

I want to take this opportunity to thank everyone who has helped to make this book a reality:

Jim Aiello, John Amplas, Atmosphere Entertainment, Rich Baderinwa, Jeanie Jefferies Brown Boshoven, Bill Cardille, Lori Cardille, Richard Catizone, Glenn Charbonneau, Mike Christopher, Michael Cucinotta, Dead Films, Inc., Death Ensemble Horror, Lawrence DeVincentz, Marilyn Eastman, David Emge, Donald Farmer, Phil Fasso, Neil Fawcett, Alex John-Feltch, Ken Foree, Michael Gornick, Vincent Guastini, Guerilla Films, Karl Hardman, Sharon Hill, Bill Hinzman, Heidi Hinzman Homepageofthedead.com, iconsoffright.com, Image Ten, Inc., Imagine, Inc., Lee Karr, John Kirch, Kevin Kriess, Jim Krut, George Kosana, Ralph Langer, The Latent Image, The Laurel Group, Laurel Entertainment, Inc., Libra Films, Leonard Lies, Living Dead Museum, Living Dead Weekend, Al Magliochetti, Market Square Productions, Dawn Michelucci, Dee Michelucci, Robert J. Michelucci, Jeff Monahan, MW Communications, Greg Nicotero, Darwin Owens, Laura Parker, Questar Magazine, Jeani Rector, Debbie Rochon, Jim Rogal, George A. Romero, Gaylen Ross, Barbara Russell, John A. Russo, Tom Savini, Marty Schiff, Kyra Schon, Gina Sestak, Joe Shelleby, Christian Stavrakis, Taso Stavrakis, Gary Streiner, Russ Streiner, Regis Survinski, Vincent Survinski, Terror Transmission, terrortransmission.com, United Film Distribution Company, Universal Pictures Corp., Westwood Artists International

DEDICATION

To George A. Romero
and all zombie creators and fans everywhere.

CONTENTS

Acknowledgements	2
Introduction by Greg Nicotero	6
Introduction II by Bob Michelucci	10
Foreword: *Memoirs of a Zombie*	11

I: NIGHT OF THE LIVING DEAD™

George A. Romero	16
Karl Hardman	47
Marilyn Eastman	50
Hardman & Eastman	52
Bill Hinzman	59
Judy O'Dea	62
Rudi Ricci	66
Vince Survinski	68
Regis Survinski	71
Kyra Schon	75
George Kosana	80
Russ Streiner	89
Gary Streiner	100

Charles Craig	113
John A. Russo	118
Richard Catizone	136

II: DAWN OF THE DEAD

Gaylen Ross	143
David Emge	149
Ken Foree	153
John Amplas	164
David Crawford	169
Taso Stavrakis	176
Mike Christopher	179
Tom Savini	192
Ralph Langer	196
Marty Schiff	213
Jim Krut	216
Randy Kovitz	224
Jeanie Jefferies	228
Michael Gornick	236
Lanny Powers	250
Leonard Lies	258
Sharon Hill	264
Joe Shelby	267

III: DAY OF THE DEAD

Howard Sherman	270
Jeff Monahan	275
Barbara Russell	282
Lori Cardille	285
Joe Pilato	291
Glenn Charbonneau	298

IV: LAND OF THE DEAD
DIARY OF THE DEAD

Greg Nicotero	306
John Harrison	319

V: NIGHT OF THE LIVING DEAD 30™
CHILDREN OF THE LIVING DEAD

Vincent Guastini	329
Heidi Hinzman	333
Dee Michelucci	340
Dawn Michelucci	345
Debbie Rochon	351

INTRODUCTION

"KNIGHT" OF THE LIVING DEAD
By Greg Nicotero
Executive Producer, Director, Special FX Make-Up

© R. Michelucci.

In the horror world, playing a zombie in a George A. Romero film is like being knighted. First and foremost, you enter a very elite brotherhood of people....many friends or business associates of "The King". Secondly, it a badge of honor.....an "undead" purple heart if you will, that bonds you together with others that have shared the same rotting foxhole. And most importantly, you get an opportunity to become a small part of horror history, having been directed by one of the most iconic and passionate directors in the world.

I owe most of my career to George, a genuine, dedicated and visionary man who single handedly changed the landscape of filmmaking....and in his way continues to do so today. NIGHT OF THE LIVING DEAD and, for me even more so, DAWN OF THE DEAD stopped me in my tracks, jaw dropped, bile rose, goosebumps erupted...in the greatest way possible.

My first zombie experience began in July 1984 when I was hired by George to work with Tom Savini on DAY OF THE DEAD. The original screenplay called for a soldier to be killed, and subsequently discovered by others as a reanimated severed head. Since we were waiting on an approved budget and shooting schedule, it was decided that I would play that zombie....YAY!!!! Then of course in the next sentence it was revealed that it would be an animatronic head lying on a table. BOOOO! I didn't get to play the zombie version of my soldier character's big moment. BUT I was excited to be able to be a part of what I knew would be a memorable moment in a horror series that so inspired me. As the weeks passed, it was determined that the budget was too high and trims needed to be made...but since we had started work producing my head this "gag" was kept in the film. However, now I had to play a part in the movie....not just be a dead head. I had dialog, blocking and got to craft a mini back story along with my onscreen cohort Taso Stavrakis. Now, as my first film....and never stepping foot in front of a movie camera let alone a movie set....I was excited, terrified, anxious and exuberant...all at the same time. I shot my scenes, hung with the actors when I wasn't flopping real guts and gore around the set, and created some amazing memories. One of my fondest involved one of shooting a scene with the entire cast in which my character was smoking and mind you, I had never smoked a cigarette in my life. When we broke for lunch George laughed when I staggered; green faced, out of my chair, put an arm around me and led me to the cafeteria. "Sorry kid."

Part of being a make-up effects artist is the intent to guarantee that each "gag" goes off without a hitch. If there is one Seminole thing I learned working with Tom Savini and George, it was the idea of anticipating what could go wrong and getting ahead of it.... because you know cleaning up 5 gallons of blood for take two is no easy task. Taking this into consideration, I donned zombie make-up to "puppeteer" the dummy head of Taso when he is attacked by zombies during the climax of DAY. I was responsible for shoving my fingers into the empty eye-sockets (rigged to bleed) and pull the head from the body tearing skin, muscle, and tendons.

CUT TO: Several years later and I had relocated to LA, opened my own make-up effects studio KNB EFX GROUP, and been fortunate enough to amass quite a resume. I received a call from George and low and behold, LAND OF THE DEAD was on the horizon. We had discussed a few projects here and there that George was attached to (RESIDENT EVIL, THE DIAMOND DEAD and LAND'S earlier incarnation DEAD RECKONING), but the chance to do another "Dead" film was my opportunity to repay George for giving me my start in the business. We prepped in the spring of 2004 and late fall shot the film in Toronto. Again, I sat for a number of the make-up tests and designed a new look for the zombies with my team that I was quite proud of. I played the

"Bridge" zombie that struggles with Simon Baker's character before being decapitated by the draw bridge, my head falling into the dark cold waters of Canada. Again, the thrill of being able to play a zombie and collaborate with George took me right back to my first days in 1984.

SURVIVAL OF THE DEAD went into production a year later and again I was asked to play a zombie.... this time a doctor feasting on a patient. George felt this particularly fitting since when we had initially met I was headed to college to study pre-med.... something he always felt bad about, robbing the world of another doctor....I sort of see it differently.

All in all some of the greatest memories I have over the last 33 years have been standing next to George while I was wearing a zombie make-up, and this book gives you a chance to experience those emotions from the perspective of a great number of friends, co-workers and fellow folks from "da burgh".

INTRODUCTION II
By Bob Michelucci

For the past forty years, fans of the living dead have asked what it was like for me to transform into a zombie for the original DAWN OF THE DEAD.

Whether interacting with diehard zombie fans at a convention question and answer session or book signing, receiving a message from a new enthusiast on social media, or reading a review of one of the myriad of recent zombie-themed television shows or movies, the interest and excitement in all things living dead, it would seem, have only intensified since the release of George A. Romero's classic, NIGHT OF THE LIVING DEAD™, forty-five years ago.

This interest and excitement, and the questions it has bred, are why I've reached out to the various undead celebrities featured in this book – some who I have had the pleasure of eating flesh with since my 1978 involvement in the Pittsburgh, Pennsylvania horror movie scene – and their live followers, to create an everything-you've-always-wanted-to-know resource for horror buffs.

I thank each of you, living or undead, for your enthusiasm in bringing this compilation to light. And I thank fans everywhere for keeping all of us zombies…alive?

Bob Michelucci
DAWN OF THE DEAD (1978)
@scopezombie

FOREWORD

MEMOIRS OF A ZOMBIE

With our offices – mine at *Questa*r magazine, and George Romero's Latent Image Studios - just a few floors from one another, it was only a matter of time before I became good friends with Mr. Romero and make-up expert Tom Savini, for the upcoming second installment in the Living Dead narrative, DAWN OF THE DEAD

In the course of a casual conversation one spring day in 1978, Mr. Romero and Tom mentioned they were looking for local extras to play zombies in DAWN. To my surprise, they asked if I would like to take a shot at, well, dying.

Having been a lifelong horror fan, it was an offer I couldn't refuse. So, at 10:30 p.m., after mall shopping hours and just before that time when the dead come out to play, I entered the Community Room in Monroeville Mall, right outside of my hometown of Pittsburgh.

After the blast   (Photo by Dee Michelucci)

At least a hundred other extras were lined up ahead of me, many of them in the process of being transformed for their zombie roles. A few of the extras that had already gone through make-up wandered in and out of the room, waiting to be called to the set. When it came my turn for make-up, Tom Savini casually asked me if I wanted to be a *special* zombie.

"Of course!" I said, without hesitation. Since my curiosity had been sparked, I then of course asked Tom what the difference was between a "special" zombie and a regular one. Tom's answer was straightforward: "You'll be shot in the forehead!" I should have known.

Later, when I had been transformed into a zombie and rigged for a special gunshot effect, I was told not to leave the room and that I would be called when they were ready to shoot the scene.

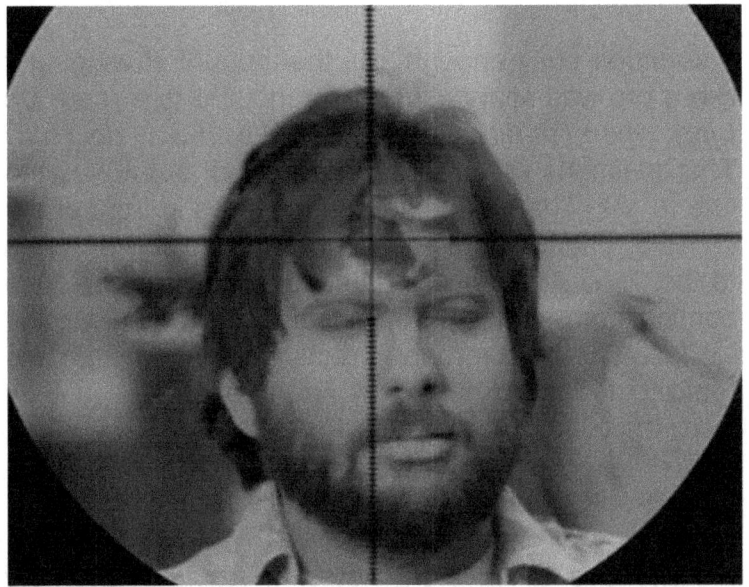

© Laurel Entertainment, Inc.

Early the next morning, the call finally came for all special zombies to report to the main shooting area on the upper level of the mall. Of course, it was 5:30 a.m., so by this time, most of us movie zombies looked (and felt) like real zombies since we hadn't slept for almost an entire day. As I prepared to shuffle out of the Community Room, I looked around one last time to see weary, gray-faced people either trying to catch a few stray winks in uncomfortable folding chairs, or slug down mugs of black coffee in order to stay awake for filming. Once we had all arrived on set,

George Romero pointed in my direction and shouted, "We're going to shoot you three first." I was number three.

When my time came, Romero offered a little practical advice. "Bob," he said, "just have a glazed look and keep your arms outstretched, then start wandering. When you hear the gunshot sound, just fall down."

It sounded easy enough, but the thought of winging it like a pro was scary. *But wait!* I thought to myself. *Do I jerk when I'm hit? Do I waver? Which way do I fall?* The questions raced through my mind, but it was too late to ask. The next thing I knew, I was in front of the camera. There was a sudden **bang!** I quickly dropped to the floor. It was over in a second. I heard applause coming from somewhere behind me. I turned around to face a large group watching the filming, and realized I was so nervous I hadn't even known they were there.

"Just great!" Romero hollered. "Let's wrap it up."

It may have taken eight hours of sitting in a lonely room with a gray face, but it was worth it—there I was, up on the silver screen for at least *six long, dramatic seconds*. Watch for me and you'll get the scope of things.

Bob Michelucci

PART ONE

NIGHT
OF THE
LIVING DEAD™

GEORGE A. ROMERO

WRITER, DIRECTOR, PRODUCER, DEITY

INTERVIEW BY LEE KARR
PART I: *BLANK OF THE DEAD*
PART II: *BEING GEORGE A. ROMERO*

© 2009 by Lee Karr

NIGHT OF THE LIVING DEAD™ (1968)
DAWN OF THE DEAD (1978)
DAY OF THE DEAD (1985)
LAND OF THE DEAD (2005)
DIARY OF THE DEAD (2007)
SURVIVAL OF THE DEAD (2010)

(© Image Ten, Inc.)

Nearly 25 years ago I became a fan of George Romero. One night, during the early summer of 1985, I was watching one of my then favorite shows, *Late Night with David Letterman*. On the show that night was a guest named Tom Savini who was on the show to plug a horror film called DAY OF THE DEAD. Before this I never watched horror films - I was 13 years old and scared to even watch the end of Jaws! Well, that appearance by Tom Savini changed all of that. I was fascinated by the effects & props and it sparked a lot of curiosity about these types of films. I went to Walden Books at my local mall a few days after this and discovered *Fangoria* issue #47 with the zombie "Dr. Tongue" on the cover. I read that issue countless times and studied the photographs from the film. This led to my renting of DAWN OF THE DEAD at a local video store and being formally introduced to the cinema of George A. Romero.

Later that fall, on Halloween night to be precise, I was fortunate enough to get the chance to see DAY OF

THE DEAD in the movie theaters. While waiting in the lobby, I can remember a girl coming out of the previous showing laughing and screaming about how gross it was. I went back several times that week to see it again and even took my uncle to one of the viewings. At the end of the film when the soldiers are eaten, he turned to me and said "Jesus Christ, what the hell did you take me to see!" I loved it! I enjoyed every minute of the film and it still remains one the best times I've ever had at the movies.

A couple of years later in 1987 I purchased the book *The Zombies That Ate Pittsburgh,* an absolute must have for any George Romero fan. By this time, I had become a full blown Romero cinephile and was as hardcore of a fan as you could find. At that time, the thought that someday I might have the chance to be a zombie in one of his films, visit one of his film sets to write an article, or sit down in his home to interview him was something that never occurred to me. Those things would never happen, and it was silly to even think of such things. However, all of those things did happen for me and they all happened in the last 5 years!

The opportunity to interview George came about because of a chance meeting after the close of the Chiller Theatre convention this past April. I was assisting john Amplas at the show and John wanted to do some catching up with George, so we went up to his room in the hotel. George, after a couple of drinks, gave me his home phone number and told me to call him whenever I wanted. He also did this because of a possible project that I am playing a very minor behind the scenes role in for George, the idea of which came about during the meeting in the hotel. This possible non-horror project is a massive long shot at best, but you never know, so we'll see what happens with it.

One day it hit me, what if I gave George a call to see if he was willing to sit down and discuss his newest film and maybe even talk about the old days in Pittsburgh as well? I'm sure George has better things to do with his day than sit down for another interview, but George was generous enough to say yes to this amateur reporter. The interview that follows is divided into two sections, with the first section dealing with the currently titled OF THE DEAD. The second section is more of a "getting to know" type of piece on George as we discuss his personal life and former collaborators as well.

(Photo courtesy Lee Karr)

PART I: *BLANK OF THE DEAD*

Walking into the lobby of the downtown Toronto apartment building that George Romero lives in and telling the man at the concierge desk that George Romero is expecting my arrival sounds so strange to me. I almost expect him to laugh and tell me to please leave. Thankfully this does not happen, and he calls up to Romero's suite and I am given the approval to head upstairs. When I arrive upstairs and find his suite, the door is already propped open for me to come in. This small gesture basically says it all about George and how welcoming of a person he truly is.

When I step inside, George greets me with a smile and a handshake. As we walk to the living room I notice a framed movie poster for THE TALES OF HOFFMAN and a framed photo of George and Simon Pegg. Then we walk into the living room and there I see an actual Muppet version of George that his girlfriend had made especially for him. George has added a cigarette to its mouth and affectionately refers to it as "Mini-Me". I also spy a Pittsburgh Steelers Russian nesting doll of QB Ben Roethlisberger that George purchased in Moscow, of all places.

After sitting down and getting situated, we dive right into the new zombie film and discuss what George's message is this time out. "It's mainly about tribalism, which I think is what is screwing the world up - tribalism, nationalism, religion -people taking sides. All of my zombie films have had a little touch of that, but this is specifically about it. It's about a feud, a long-standing feud between these two old guys on an island, where it should be safe and it's away from most of the chaos that's happening on the mainland. But these two old guys can't stop shooting at each other and that's more important - the feud is more important to them than trying to address the crisis." He pauses and then continues on this theme. "It's any of these wars that are based on old standing rivalries, whether they're religious, political, family, whatever. It's specifically about that." Ironically, just after George finishes, his cat Hamilton becomes entrenched in a stare down with George's bird. So even in the Romero abode, factions just can't come together it seems.

Even before DIARY OF THE DEAD was released in February of 2008, there was talk of a sequel. Reports on the internet were saying that it was going to be a direct sequel, something Romero flirted with briefly. "There was never going to be a direct sequel. There was a brief moment where I wanted to follow the three survivors in DIARY that wind up in the panic room, and I actually started to write a script, but I got off it really quickly. I've never done a really direct sequel like that, with the same main characters. So it is a bit of a sequel, in that it takes minor characters from DIARY and follows them to this island." Romero is already thinking ahead though for further adventures with his peripheral characters from DIARY OF THE DEAD, mainly because his "money people" want more of these films. "You know DIARY had a small theatrical release. It did great financially on DVD worldwide. These guys keep wanting to make them and I have to do them. They have the right - if I don't do them - they have the right to do it themselves, so I'd rather do them. So I have this idea of taking minor characters - if there's another one after this, I'll take another minor character, probably the black guy from DIARY and take him somewhere and maybe wind up with three or four films that are a pretty good description of what the world is like." He continues, "Given the fact that these guys seem to want to keep making them, I just didn't know what else to do. You can't really find new themes in the world quickly; the world doesn't change that much that fast!" When George talks about his "money people", he is speaking of Artfire Films, who also bankrolled DIARY OF THE DEAD. "Even though we're partners with them in these, we still retain ownership of the films; they call the shots because they write the checks. They don't have any creative control in the film, but they have all the business controls. Once I'm finished with the movie they can make decisions - distribution decisions - things like that." He continues, "They're great, I mean they're great partners, but I probably wouldn't want to do these this quickly, rapid fire. But I like this idea; I'd love to do maybe three or four films. We own them for the first time; well we own a piece of them with Artfire. I don't have any ownership in any of the older ones. It's nice to finally have a little piece of the action!" This last line George delivers in his best

Marlon Brando as THE GODFATHER voice, something George loves to do.

(Photo courtesy Lee Karr)

As of this interview, George still has no idea what the title of the film will be and did not seem concerned with the issue at all. In fact, it could be a case where he will not even name it himself. "Well the distributor always has the right to choose a title." he says. Romero feels that this film will probably go the same route as DIARY OF THE DEAD and premiere at the Toronto International Film Festival Midnight Madness event and most likely get released sometime in early 2010. He likes the idea of potential distributors bidding on the film, increasing the chances of a better deal. During this topic, out of the blue, George also drops in a tease regarding "zombie rules" and that something unexpected happens in this newest film. I have a feeling that a lot of fans might already know what this unexpected happening involving the "zombie rules" is.

During my set visit back in November of 2008, several key members of the production used the term "western" to describe the film, and George agrees. "It's not really a theme, it's a flavor that I just wanted to put on this film and I could do it because they're off on this island and there's no cars and they're all on horseback, so I pushed it a little bit and I just went a little further with the western thing."

In a recent *USA TODAY* article, Romero was quoted as saying that this one would be closer to DAWN OF THE DEAD as far as action goes, but he softens that a bit. "To the extent that if you had to say that DIARY was close to one of my other zombie films, it was closest to NIGHT. Initially I was thinking well this is going to be a little closer to DAWN, because it's more colorful and it's narrative and there is more action in it, but not a tremendous amount. It's not like DAWN, it's not like a romp in the park, fun all the way - this is a little heavier. But it's definitely more action than DIARY and it's more of a "story". And it's not subjective camera, except for little pieces of it that sort of wrap around. That's the way I would do them all."

One of the biggest reasons that Romero's films have resonated with fans are the characters. He has always had a knack for creating colorful and complex characters that are usually at odds with one another.

"Well the main characters, the heroes if you want to call them that, are the four national guardsmen. They're the guys we get into the movie with. But there's a back story on the island and it's about these two old guys that have been feuding since kindergarten - it's the Muldoon's and the O'Flynn's! A couple of little surprises, I don't want to - well I can't give them away, they're too...well they're too important. I'll tell you, but you got to keep it a secret. You think he has a daughter. When you see the island in a flashback in the beginning of the movie, he's got a daughter - O'Flynn is the guy. O'Flynn believes we should go around and kill the dead - seems to make sense (laughing). Muldoon is sort of a religious fanatic, who says you want to kill our sisters, our brothers, our children - maybe somebody will find a cure for this. So he believes in keeping them chained up and hoping for the best. He thinks it might be a virus, it might be something curable. They're sort of back woods people. So in addition to all the old stuff that they used to feud about, now they have this new issue. Muldoon kind of gets the drop on O'Flynn at some point and is going to kill him and O'Flynn's daughter intervenes and say's why don't we just send him off, we'll put him on a boat, get rid of him - so they ship him off the island. They don't want any strangers on the island, so O'Flynn makes it his point to send strangers. He gets this abandoned little boat shed in a pier in Delaware on the mainland. He's renting boats and telling people -he actually goes on the internet and say's 'come on out to Plum Island, it's safe out here!' So he's sending people out there to annoy Muldoon and then of course our guys hook up with him." It's here that I have to stop. Unfortunately, I cannot divulge the rest of what George has to say, simply because I gave my word to keep it a secret. Sorry guys.

For the score this time around, George originally turned to an old friend in John Harrison. John's scores for CREEPSHOW and DAY OF THE DEAD are very memorable, so it was exciting news when it was announced that he was returning to create the music for this film. Unfortunately, now that will not be the case. "No, he's gotten too busy. He hasn't done a score for a long time and was a little nervous about it in the first place, but he did a sample. He did the first reel and I thought the stuff was beautiful. He would have had to hire a producer and a studio, and the equipment, because he doesn't have it at home - he doesn't have the production facilities. He can't really get all the voices and make it sound less "synthy". And he lost a big job and needed to hustle to get something else going, because he wasn't going to make any money on this, so he decided to bail. Too bad, we had our spotting sessions, we were hanging out - you know, I love John from years and years of hanging out with him. I felt really bad when he bailed, because the work that he did was really great." According to George the film does have a new composer, Robert Carli, who has worked with the Toronto Symphony and teaches at the University of

Toronto. Carli has done film scores for Canadian feature films and television films, and George seemed pleased with what he has heard so far.

DIARY OF THE DEAD was very different from his past efforts. The subjective camera work and young cast gave a new flavor to the series. Besides the western theme, can the fans look forward to something a little different this time around? "No (laughs). As I say there's a little bit of subjective camera in the beginning and if I do this collection - if I wind up doing a couple more of these I would start it that way, just in deference to DIARY. I sort of like that connection. The opening shot is Alan Van Sprang on a subjective camera. Now, that's the way it's playing. The problem is all this shit can change within the next few weeks. We saved all of that to use now, so that we can go thru the film and see if there were any other places where we could use a little bit of narration or throw them in to help the story, same thing we did with DIARY. We did all the narration after everything else was done, so that you could watch the movie and say well this is a little unclear, maybe we can bring in a shot of that to explain it. It's a trick, it's a device, but it works pretty well. It helps you glue it all together."

Besides the social and political allegory in his films, one of the biggest trademarks of George's work is the gore. He held back a great deal with DIARY OF THE DEAD, showing very little. How will this newest one compare? "It's restrained compared to DAY or DAWN,

I mean it has to be these days because it has to be R, nobody is going to put it out un-rated. It certainly has more than DIARY and there's one really sort of spectacular sequence, but we're worried whether the MPAA will allow it - where they pull a guy apart, a bit reminiscent of Pilato. But it's at night, it's darker - I hope we can get away with it. You know, it's always how do you kill these guys, and it's always about coming up with interesting or funny ways of getting rid of one of these guys. There's a bunch of that and some of them are funnier than they are gory. I think some of them are pretty incredible, if I say so myself." George excuses himself to the kitchen to pour a drink and continues, "There's a hell of a lot of gun play. Everybody say's oh man, you're just shooting them now, but I bet if you go back to DAWN, 85% of the kills in DAWN are gunshots. It's the fastest way, most logical way, if you have a gun. Not everybody has a helicopter (laughs).

Unlike the last two zombie films, George say's not to expect any famous cameos or voice-overs this time around. He also wishes that the film would go directly to video, making it easier for the fans to access it. The film, which was shot digitally on The Red One camera, was a very challenging experience for the sixty-nine year old film maker. "I loved the experience, except that we got *KILLED* by weather, I mean we just got killed. We weren't able to shoot all of the scenes that were in the script because we were just killed by weather. There was one big zombie scene that I would have loved to have gotten, but we just ran out of time- I mean we got snow, rain - we lost about three and a half days to weather, on a twenty-five day schedule."

Recently an online trailer for the film was released by Voltage Pictures, stirring up debate among fans. As some suspected, Romero was not involved with its release. "We weren't aware of it until it appeared and then people started calling up and saying wow it looks great (Romero shrugs his shoulders). Everybody hit the roof, I mean skyrockets went off, because they have no right to do it - Voltage had no right to do that. They're sales agents, the materials they were getting from us were supposed to be exclusively for selling to European distributors, and they shouldn't have put it online. It was not color corrected, there were zombies dying with no blood flying, none of the effects were in it...it's bad and that kind of shit can kill you. You know, it's like these kids that somehow rip it off and your movie gets reviewed before it's even out of the lab. Some asshole at the lab lets out a work print or something - people have it and it's getting reviewed and people are saying it's garbage, don't go to see it! You're dead before you start, it's awful, I mean it's terrible."

Fans expectations for Romero's films are always extremely high and you can never meet those standards for some, but what kind of expectations does he have himself? "I don't think it will be as exciting, DIARY had this unique quality to it and this one I'm not sure does. I like it a lot, but it doesn't have that flavor – DIARY had this unique thing with the subjective camera and all that. Nobody knew about Cloverfield, when we were making it nobody knew about Cloverfield, that other people were doing it. But it had that touch of, some people called it, sophistication and it got good reviews. I think this film will get - my shit always gets mixed reviews - but I think this will get its share of good reviews. The acting is terrific and there's obviously a point to it. But I don't know if...you know we just have to wait and see."

Before closing I wanted to see if George might have a message for the fans and I honestly expected a typical response that encompassed some thanks and appreciation but George, as Peter Grunwald had told me on the set, is unpredictable and gave an honest and blunt message to all of us. "Basically, what I want

George Romero signing autographs at the 1993 Zombie Jamboree (Photo by Bob Michelucci)

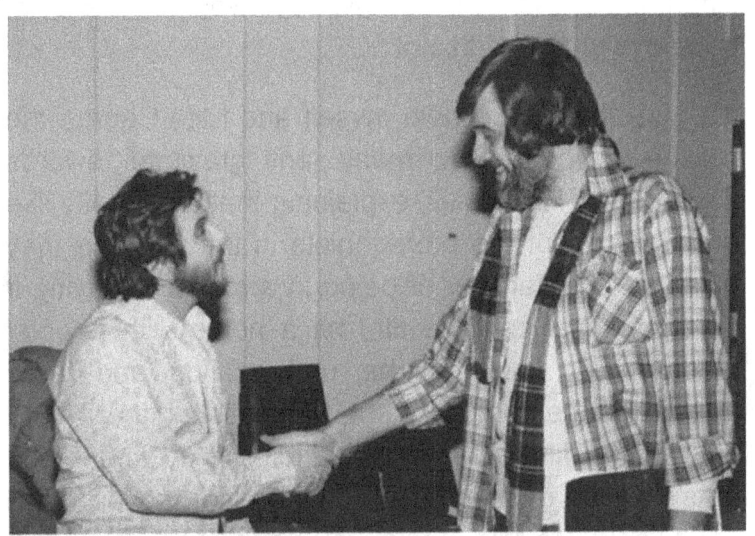
Meeting with George Romero (Photo courtesy Bob Michelucci)

to say is forgive me. I guess the basic thing that bugs me, the biggest thing that bugs me is that fans want me to do either the last movie I did or do another DAWN or do another this or do another that - and that pisses me off! That's not what I'm about! I'm gonna make a movie; look at it, if you don't like it that's fine. If you like it, then I love it. In other words, don't punish me because this was not as good as DAWN. This is what I'm thinking right now, I'm making this movie right now, this is what I'm thinking, give it a break! Look at it, maybe it will take you two or three times to look at it, but look at it. All I can say is that I'm trying my best and don't punish me because it's not as "good" as DAWN, because DAWN was not even "good", it was fun, but it wasn't "good". I think this new movie, Blank of the dead, is much better in a cinematic sense than DAWN, but I worry that a lot of people might think it's not."

It's here that I can't help myself and I tell George the reason why I feel so many fans gravitate towards DAWN OF THE DEAD, explaining that they really like and care about the protagonists in the film and they also love that fantasy of being in a mall and having it all to themselves. The film hit a nerve with people! George tells me that he understands and does appreciate the sentiment but, "I'm satisfied that what I did with this film is what I would I like to do with it. The fans may be expecting something else, maybe not, I don't know. It's this magic, you don't know. You work on a film, you work on it in a bubble, and you're completely in a bubble. Here's the movie - I like this, I like this, I like this, you shape it, you make it what you want it to be. Now you kick it out there and all of a sudden people either like it or they don't. I've never been an A list guy, I didn't do huge movies. I'm grateful that I'm still around doing these little movies, but even doing little movies somebody bombs you! It's really frustrating, it's very frustrating to sit there and you know exactly what you're doing, and you're doing things within a budget. You're not going to compete with the big movies of the time; I can't compete with the big shit that's out there. And you hope that at least your fans will come around and say 'Woo, cool man we're with you still'. Except that even your fans, even the 19 fans that you have are split. 19 doesn't split evenly, so it's 10 - 9 liking it, not liking it. C'mon boys,

I mean I did this, this was the idea that I had, and I did it. C'mon stick with me."

Editor's Note: PART 1: *BLANK OF THE DEAD* was released in 2010 under the title *SURVIVAL OF THE DEAD*

PART II: *BEING GEORGE A. ROMERO*

The view from George Romero's top floor apartment balcony is a great one, especially for a film location geek. If you look to the north you can see a section of town that a lot of Bruiser was shot in and if you look to the northeast you can see the top of Filmport Studios where some of his latest film was shot, plus the Cherry Street drawbridge from LAND OF THE DEAD as well. One bad thing about being so high up though is that the wind can take your plants and flowers and send them flying, as Romero found out very recently, and we won't even mention the table umbrella that became a helicopter one night. Back inside I can hear what sounds like the laundry dryer going and this gets me to wondering, what does a horror legend do during his off time? What's a typical day in the life of George Romero like? "Well you just walked in on one... I'm trying to work a peace deal between the cat and the bird, mostly (laughs). When Susan is around we play Scrabble. When you leave I'm going to have to write some more." George is in the middle of writing some new scenes for OF THE DEAD that he and producer Peter Grunewald have brain stormed over a period of several days. "See this is what happens, Peter comes in for three days and we beat out this stuff! Peter dutifully types it while were talking and he sends me these reminders of what we talked about. It's great you know, but now I have to make somebody actually say this shit."

When George mentions Susan, he is referring to his girlfriend, whom he met during the production of LAND OF THE DEAD. They live in the St. Lawrence Market area of Toronto and enjoy a low key, no frills life style. "We bought track lighting this weekend and put it up. It's a completely normal life! I go to movies, I watch Turner Classics mostly. I have a very simple life, I like simple things. I don't want rich things, I don't care. Love to travel - this was Memorial Day in the U.S. and I completely forgot, because up here, last weekend was Queen Victoria Day, or whatever the hell it was. I swear Canadians have more holidays than Americans, which is also a good reason to be up here (laughs). We went to Lake Huron, we hung out, we got a little cottage, there was no one around, and did a jigsaw puzzle. I mean this is the shit that I love to do." He continues, "You know Scene It, this game Scene It, the movie game? We have all the editions of that and we're at the point where we know it already by heart, we need a new edition. Luckily, Sus loves board games, I love board games, and we hang out. We have a great time together - she's great, she's really terrific. We're just regular guys."

I was surprised to learn that George really does not watch a lot of news or listen to talk radio, considering how political his films are. "There are only two things that are ever on TV when I'm home alone. It's either CNN, which I go to only if there's a shit movie on Turner Classics, otherwise it's Turner. It's Turner all the time, except when Fred and Ginger come on I switch over to CNN (laughs)." He continues, "It becomes wall paper - I can write, I can do anything. Mainly it's write, that's all I ever do here. If I'm sitting home alone, I'm either writing on a deadline or I'm writing for the fun of it and it never bothers me. I probably steal lines, without knowing it (laughs)." Another thing that I discovered about George is that he enjoys spending time in the kitchen. "I love cooking; it just really takes the world away. It takes the world away completely."

Contrary to many reports on the internet and in magazines, Romero is not a Canadian citizen. He is considered a permanent resident of Canada but is still a U.S. citizen. He also is currently working out a divorce agreement with his long-time wife Christine. I asked him about his new life in the great white north. "It's really not very different at all; I think I'm the same guy. I don't know if Chris got tired of me or I got tired of her, whatever happened there I don't even want to go into that, so I don't know. I love Sus, I'm the same guy, my kids come up and visit, you know, so I don't feel a big difference at all." He cites his daughter Tina, who is studying to become a film maker herself, as the one thing that he is most proud of in his life. "I hope she really wants to do it and isn't doing it just to follow in the footsteps. She's very talented, she's really good."

George grew up in The Bronx in New York and was raised Catholic. He talked about his Latino heritage and how his own Father held certain prejudices against Latinos. "I'm half Latino, I'm a New York baby right. So my Dad is Cuban, my Mom is Lithuanian. My Dad say's 'I'm not Cuban!'(George shrugs his shoulders) - but you were born in Cuba? 'I am Castilian, from Spain! Family went to Cuba to open a hotel!' Okay, well let's say you're a Cuban, you're a Spanish guy? 'Yes, but I am not a Puerto Rican!' I grew up in New York with a Spanish Dad right in the days of WEST SIDE STORY, where you know the Puerto Rican gangs and shit? My Dad is telling me Puerto Ricans are shit. I have a Latino Dad who's telling me that Puerto Ricans are shit. (Laughs) I mean this is a very confusing situation...anyway."

Listening to George tell stories is a blast. He shared so many different little anecdotes "off the record", that it kills me not to include them in this piece. He told stories of former colleagues that were both hilarious and jaw dropping at the same time. He shared the story of his childhood competition in New York with Martin Scorsese in renting a print of THE TALES OF HOFFMAN. "When we finally met, we never met back then, but we knew who we were, because we were the only guys that were renting The Tales of Hoffmann! I didn't meet him til way later, I mean way after, even after GOODFELLAS, was the first time I met him. And I said, you son-of-a-bitch! And he said YOU son-of-a-bitch! (Laughs)" He spoke about finally meeting his hero Michael Powell, who directed THE TALES OF HOFFMANN, thru his encounter with Scorsese and how exciting it was for him. He credits the director and the film with making him want to make movies. George truly loves and respects the film and is even interviewed on the Criterion DVD release.

He also spoke about another legendary film maker, Dario Argento. "When I first met Dario Argento he was really powerful, he was a powerful guy. He could do anything he wanted; he was the Spielberg of Italy or one of them, one of the top names in Italy. So he could wake up in the morning and say I'm not going to shoot today because I've changed my mind about that scene and he could get away with that. I've never done that! I've never shown up and said guys go home."

One really fascinating story that George shared was about the casting of the Barbara character in the original NIGHT OF THE LIVING DEAD™ and how Fred Rogers changed living dead history. "Nobody knows this I don't think; I've never seen it in print. Remember Lady Aberlin on the original *Mister Rogers' Neighborhood*? Her real name was Betty Aberlin, a Pittsburgh actress, and I thought she was the best actress in town. So when we were casting for Night of the living dead I called up Betty, because I knew Chef Brockett and all the cast that were on that show, and so they gave me Betty's number and I called Betty and said 'you want to make this movie, we're gonna make this movie here' (in full Marlon GODFATHER Brando voice), and she said yes! And Fred said no. My old buddy Fred said I can't let Lady Aberlin be in a horror movie and that's why Judy O'Dea got it."

The longer my conversation with George went, and the more "truth serum" he downed, a side came out of him that surprised me a little. I've always known that he is an extremely humble man and is almost uncomfortable with people heaping praise upon him. At one point he tells me not to be more impressed with him than he is with himself. He is very critical of his work and I got the feeling that perhaps he thought his success was just luck. "It's not that special! I look at a cheeseburger B-movie on Turner and whoever made that movie was more professional and did a better job than I did on Night. Yet all of a sudden, I get these accolades for NIGHT. I know why - there was a black guy, there was social commentary, I know why - but the movie is not that well made. It is not well made AT ALL!" He continues, "I didn't know how to make a movie. I was telling a story and I had a couple of radical ideas and, you know, it's more of a political statement than it is a film. Bruiser was the first film where I felt that I really knew what I was doing and that's like, Christ, my eleventh or twelfth film. I really felt that I know, I think I know how to control this now a little bit."

For the last twenty years Romero has worked with producer Peter Grunwald and their working relationship has lasted twice as long as his former partnership with Richard Rubinstein. I was curious as to how the two compared. "Well it's very different, first of all Peter's a good friend (laughs). Richard was a friend - I still talk to him and we still sort of get along - but he was a real hard driving, business kind of guy. Peter is half me; I mean he's half creative. He's a wonderful story editor, he cares about the story, and he cares about the film itself. Richard was the kind of guy, who would, and I don't mean this to cut Richard down, but he was the kind of guy who would say 'oh I give George all the freedom in the world' - but it was only because he wasn't interested. I could never sit down with Richard for two days straight, forty-eight solid hours, with no sleep and talk story, and try to map it out and all that. Peter's game for all of that stuff, so that's wonderful. He's very smart and he's very good at business - he's probably not as aggressive as Richard was, but that's fine with me too. I don't like sharks, I'm a not a good enough swimmer (laughs)."

Much like he did in his Pittsburgh days, Romero is building a "family" in the Toronto film community. People such as cinematographer Adam Swica, costume designer Alex Kavanagh, and actor Alan Van Sprang all are now Romero film veterans. Romero doesn't just prefer to work with people he knows and trusts, he needs to. "You really need a relationship with the key people - A.D., script supervisor, director of photography most importantly, and the editor probably even more importantly." He continues, "So I wound up meeting a whole bunch of new people. It's just hard, it's hard to start up a relationship with somebody fresh and try to explain - you get to meet the DP three days before you go to camera. You don't have time to sit down and get drunk and talk about what you want to do. Tony Roberts, on *The Dark Half*, thought he was going to win an Oscar for something, actually took off and went out to the Oscars for a week and we had to work with another guy. Because of that, he thought that he was the most important person on the set. We had huge fights over ridiculous things; anyway, I won't go into that."

Romero feels that he had nothing to do with the creation of a viable film community in Pittsburgh. He feels that FLASHDANCE was responsible for opening the eyes of Hollywood to Pittsburgh and it in turn brought many productions to Western Pennsylvania.

During our long, nearly three-hour talk, I decided to have a little fun with one of the most clichéd things you can do...word association. Of course, this was simply impossible for George to do though. First up, Richard Rubinstein - "It ain't a word, it's hard. That's a ten-year relationship that you can't sum up in a word. I wound up thinking differently than he thought, I'm still friendly with him - we're just different. Different! You want one word, different." George also spoke about Rubinstein's 3-D project involving the original DAWN OF THE DEAD. "I loved it! I loved the footage that I saw. Richard gracefully invited me and my daughter, when I happened to be in New York, to look at a test screening of this. I was completely blown away! Apparently, it's gonna take a long time to completely do it, but man it was beautiful. The colors were exact; the 3-D was not cookie cutter. When Ken points the rifle...outside the airport, you see the entire rifle. It's not a pop-up book, it's real. I'm blown away these technicians can actually do this. I loved it, I thought it looked gorgeous. I said 'hey Richard, this is going to be a whole new revival of this movie'. I don't know if the movie is important enough to make a big deal out of releasing it? The 3-D is unbelievable! I'm sitting here telling you it's unbelievable!"

Next, Tom Savini - "Tom was responsible for much of my success because he would invent things on the spot that are still talked about in the movies that we did."

Next, Greg Nicotero - "Greg Nicotero - long hair (Laughs)... Nobody will understand this, but I will say Alfredo's." George is referring to a chance meeting Nicotero had with Romero at a restaurant in Rome, Italy while he was a kid vacationing with his parents.

Next, Vince Survinski - "Vince Survinski was a saint! He was the guy that built a bridge, a little bridge across a little stream - enough for cars to get across, that got us to the house where we shot NIGHT OF THE LIVING DEAD™. He used to own a roller rink and said 'oh, I like showing people a good time...you gonna make movies? Well I like a certain kind of movie, I like outdoor movies.' The guy was just a simple, plain man...he went to church every day, he'd come to work every day at Latent Image. He'd park his car and walk over to St. Mary's, or whatever that downtown church is, and go to mass and then come back. At the same time he had this semi-violent streak in him. If he saw a pigeon on the sidewalk he would drive on the sidewalk to kill the fucking pigeon! This guy was a complete dichotomy, but none the less, basically a saint. Listen, I could write a novel about Vince Survinski. I cannot answer this question in a few words. This guy was one of the most extraordinary men I've ever known. I would say next to Fred Rogers, this is odd, I'd put Fred on the top of people that I know who were selfless and helped other people and had a dedication. I'd put Fred way at the top, above anybody I've ever known, and Vince is the second."

Next, Joe Pilato - "Joe Pilato! Gimme a break, how can I say anything bad about Joe, because I love Joe - even though I don't enjoy Joe (laughs). He knows this, I still see Joe, he was over there at Chiller. I love Joe; I want him to always be there. Here's the thing, what you want is for these people to always be there. Unfortunately, you get to my age and people stop being there. I want Joe to be there longer than me at least, so that he's always there! There are certain people you want them to be there longer than you, so that when you leave their still around. Joe is one of those guys."

Next, John Russo - "I love John, I still love John. John is the most practical guy - you can have a conversation with John about anything, politics, and movies, whatever. Anything he says you may not agree with it, but he's got a practical approach to it...and therefore you can never defeat his arguments, even though you would like to! I just wish John would cut a couple of chords and loosen himself up a little bit. I think he is too strict on himself and he chooses a business approach. I think he could have been a superstar, but he took the safer route. He bet the red-black, instead of ever putting it on number 17."

© Image Ten, Inc

Next, John Amplas - "John is one of the sweetest men I've ever known. I thought when he went to New York he was going to be discovered by Bob Fosse or Mike Nichols or somebody. I thought John was the most talented actor I'd ever seen and a particular angelic sort of type. He had a wonderful look, he had a wonderful presence. I don't know whether he never got an agent, I don't know what happened. I don't know why John never made it, but I think if the right guy had seen John, he would have been..." He continues, "What a talent, John is a huge talent, and yet he's not an identifiable type. He's somewhere between, I can't even think of what he's between, but he's somewhere between!"

Next, Ed Harris - "I think Ed is maybe the greatest American actor of all time! I also think that Ed is a beautiful person. You go to Ed's house for dinner and he makes you hold hands and he say's grace. I mean this guy is the most gracious, wonderful guy in the world." He continues, "The scene with him on the bicycle in Pollock where he's trying to open the f**king beer. Not only does that deserve an Oscar, it deserves a Purple Heart! He's unbelievable...Ed is sometimes unbelievable in the shit that he does."

Another former colleague that we discussed was cinematographer Mike Gornick and probably the most interesting stories that George told revolved around him. Most of them I have to leave out, due to George asking me to turn the recorder off when he told them. "He's a priest! I could probably, if had his phone number, I could call him right now and tell him that you were up here and you got a flat and you have this very peculiar kind of car that nobody can fix, except him...and he would come up! He'd be here as long as it took him to drive from Pittsburgh, he would be here! He's a priest, but sometimes he's not." One story that we spoke about with Gornick, that I was allowed to record for some reason, was the mystery of the missing long version of MARTIN and the rumors that Gornick was the one who took the print from the Laurel offices in downtown Pittsburgh. I asked George if that story made any sense at all to him and he said that it did, because Gornick did not like some of the shots. Of course nobody knows anything for sure, so it remains a mystery to this day and will probably stay that way.

As the interview winds down, George wants to go grab some dinner, but I'm forced to do the unthinkable and say no. It's getting late and I have a five-hour drive ahead of me back to Pittsburgh and I have to be at work the next day. Plus, the thought of trying to squeeze a man the size of Romero into the car I was using and then driving around Toronto looking for a good restaurant struck me as a lengthy and time consuming process, so I wimped out. The time I did spend with George though was incredibly fun and filled with very memorable moments. Seeing him laugh out loud at my Billy Bob Thornton impersonation of Carl from Sling Blade doing Ken Foree's famous speech from DAWN OF THE DEAD, about there being no more room in hell, comes to mind right away. He even joked that he would write a part for me in his next movie.

There is no way to put into words what an honor it was for me to be able to spend the time I did with George. This is a man who is responsible for films that are burned into my mind's eye forever and I sat in his home where he treated me like he had known me for years.

KARL HARDMAN

MARCH 22, 1927 – SEPTEMBER 22, 2007

**ACTOR, INVESTOR, CO-PRODUCER,
SOUND EFFECTS & MUSIC CREATOR,
STILL PHOTOGRAPHER**

INTERVIEW EXCERPT FROM
QUESTAR MAGAZINE
OCTOBER 1980

NIGHT OF THE LIVING DEAD™ (1968)
"HARRY COOPER"

©Image Ten, Inc

"I have been saddened by the fact that many millions were made on this film classic and those of us in the circle of ten who launched the production have received but a few thousand dollars each. We were soundly fleeced by the distributor."

"I have been continually embarrassed by people thinking that I'm on easy street because of the success of this film. They really don't believe that I could be so stupid as to let the rewards slip through my fingers."

"I'm bitter because so much reward, gratification and fame slipped away, in part due to my own inattention. I'm cynical to the extreme about all seemingly "good deals" and in a legal system which appears to be motivated (at least in part) by whim, incredible bureaucracy, and a generous sprinkling of ineptitude."

"I'm a lot wiser! A lot of what has impacted on me in the last twelve years will never happen again."

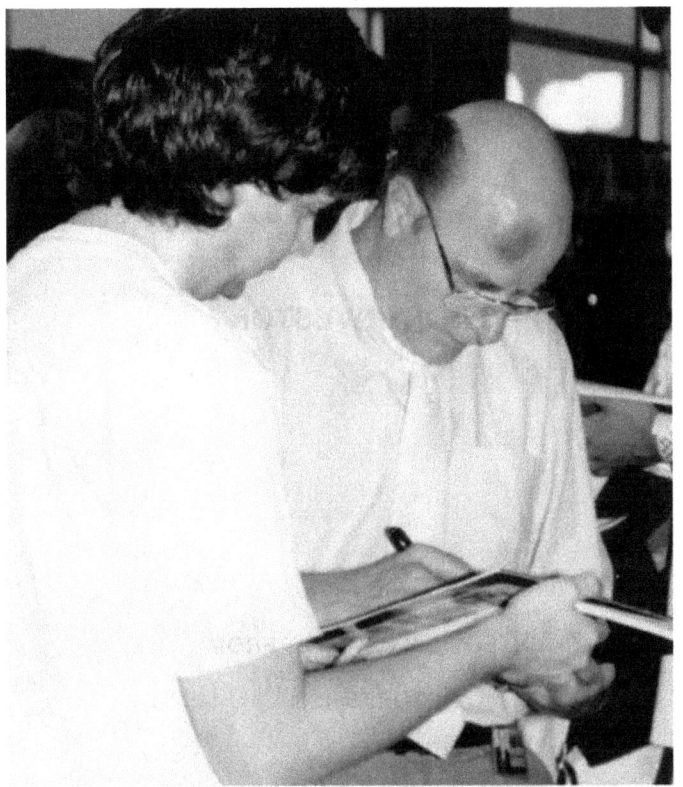

Karl signing an autograph for a fan   (Photo by Bob Michelucci)

"I'm happy to have been part of NIGHT OF THE LIVING DEAD™; to have helped create, along with nine other talented people, a classic that will outlive me."

MARILYN EASTMAN

ACTOR, INVESTOR

INTERVIEW EXCERPT FROM
***QUESTAR* MAGAZINE**
OCTOBER 1980

NIGHT OF THE LIVING DEAD™ *(1968)*
"HELEN COOPER"

©Image Ten, Inc.

"My participation in NIGHT OF THE LIVING DEAD™ made me grateful to be an American…where some of the streets are still paved in gold. NIGHT was a freak and a Cinderella. "Let's get a barn and put on a show." The film was a success. We were not. That was our fault. I relish the memories, but I wouldn't make the same mistakes again. Ego goeth before a fall. Try paying the rent with ego."

Marilyn signing an autograph for a fan
(Photo by Bob Michelucci)

KARL HARDMAN
&
MARILYN EASTMAN

INTERVIEW BY LEE KARR
PART I: *BLANK OF THE DEAD*
PART II: *BEING GEORGE A. ROMERO*

© October 2007 by Homepage of the Dead

NIGHT OF THE LIVING DEAD™ (1968)
"HARRY COOPER"
"HELEN COOPER"

©Image Ten, Inc.

What were you doing prior to NIGHT OF THE LIVING DEAD™ and how did you both get involved in the film?

Prior to NOLD, I was president of Hardman Associates Inc. and Marilyn was Vice President and Creative Director. Our firm was deeply involved in the creation and production of industrial films. The majority of our industrial clients were multi-national corporations. In addition to film work, we also created and produced and presented exhibit shows all over the world. At the time of NOLD, we had just ended a morning radio show which we broadcast from our own studios in Pittsburgh, Pennsylvania. It was a four-hour, five day a week comedy show mixed with music, news, weather reports and lots of commercials. The show was successful, but it was exhausting us. During this period, Hardman Associates employed 25 people. We had an art department, three audio recording studios, a photographic studio for commercial work, a color film processing lab for professional photographers and an

53

educational division which produced materials for use in school systems throughout the U.S.

Karl and Marilyn together at a convention (Photo by Bob Michelucci)

We had some friends who ran a small film production company by the name of The Latent Image. They produced commercials for TV. Those people were George Romero, Russell Streiner and John Russo. We had worked together on several film projects.

One day (shortly after we had ended the radio show), Marilyn received a phone call (I think it was from Russ), who said they would like to talk to us about an idea. She told him that we were very interested and the three of them came up to our studio and we sat and talked about the idea...a horror film...no title of course at that time,...and would we be interested in becoming part of a core group for the production of the film. Marilyn and I had just ended the radio show and we were ready for anything!!

That's how it all began. We became two of the ten core group. The core became Image Ten Inc. Today, along with Russ Streiner and John Russo, I am a trustee of Image Ten Inc., elected by the shareholders to oversee the ongoing affairs of the corporation.

NIGHT OF THE LIVING DEAD™ is generally considered a revolutionary film for its time. When you read the script what were your initial reactions to it?

When we read the script initially, the five of us agreed that it would take a goodly amount of work to make it really horrific. George's idea was excellent, we thought. John said that he would go to work on the screen play and the dialogue for Helen and Harry Cooper in the basement sequences would be written by Marilyn.

And so it began to evolve.

In regard to it being a revolutionary film...yes, it certainly was...but that was accidental. We knew that we could not raise enough money to shoot a film on a par with the classic horror films with which we had all grown up. The best that we could do was to place our cast in a remote spot and then bring the horror to be visited on them in that spot. We had no idea that we would be creating a mutation of the horror film genre. Our goal: "make it as scary as we could."

There have been references that have said the script was being written by John Russo as the film was being made. Is this true and if so to what extent? Did you have any input?

The references to the script being written while we were shooting the film, came about largely, I believe, because of the lead actor, Duane Jones. The script had been written with the character Ben as a rather simple truck driver. His dialogue was that of a lower class/uneducated person. Duane Jones was a very well educated man. He was fluent in a number of languages and went on to hold a professorship at Vassar. Duane simply refused to do the role as it was written. As I recall, I believe that Duane himself upgraded his own dialogue to reflect how he felt the character should present himself.

In the making of many films, quite often there will be dialogue changes for a variety of reasons. This task fell to John...who handled it well. Marilyn made changes in our basement dialogue as those scenes were shot.

In addition to acting I believe you were involved in other aspects of the production of the film?

As to our roles in the production: I (Karl) chose the music for the film since Hardman Associates owned the Capital film music library. I chose a selection of music for each of the various scenes and then George made the final selections. I then, took those selections and augmented them electronically.

Marilyn and I recorded all of the live sound effects used in the film (two 10-inch reels of edited tape). Marilyn was in charge of all makeup (she sure used a lot of morticians wax on the ghouls!). Wardrobe also fell to Marilyn.

Note: *Of all the sound effects that we created, the one that still gives me goose bumps when I hear it, is Marilyn's screaming as she is killed by her daughter. Judy O'Dea's screaming is a close second. Both were looped in and out of echo over and over again.*

Finally, all of the production stills for the film were shot by me and printed by me. A number of cast members formed a production line in the darkroom for developing, washing and drying of the prints as I made the exposures. As I recall, I shot over 1250 pictures during the production.

When the film was finally released many critics condemned it. What were your thoughts regarding the completed film?

When the film was finished and then condemned, we were hopeful that the condemnation would spark box office activity. Frankly, we were all too close to the film to realize just how frightening it really was. It took months for us to accept the fact that it really did scare people!

Karl, a strange twist was that Harry was actually right; the cellar was the safest place. Does this get mentioned often?

Yes, Harry was correct regarding the basement. To this day, people come up to me and say, "I hated you in that movie.....but you were right about the basement".

In what way has NIGHT affected your lives?

NOLD has not had a tremendous effect on our lives. However, for the past thirty years, we have lived, almost daily, with reminders of the film...most often via mail from fans (mail seems to be increasing...notably from young people who have been captivated by the film), or from people we meet on the street. There are increasing requests from fans who want to know if we have anything to sell!?!? As a consequence, we have indeed begun to produce items for sale. Perhaps the most important effect the film has had for us...on us, is the profound feeling that the fans of NOLD have engendered in us. We are humbled by our fans!

BILL HINZMAN

OCTOBER 24, 1936 – FEBRUARY 5, 2012

ACTOR, INVESTOR, DIRECTOR, CINEMATOGRAPHER

INTERVIEW EXCERPT FROM *QUESTAR* MAGAZINE
OCTOBER 1980

NIGHT OF THE LIVING DEAD™ (1968)
FLESHEATER (1988)
NIGHT OF THE LIVING DEAD 30™ (1998)

"CEMETARY ZOMBIE"

©Image Ten, Inc.

"NIGHT OF THE LIVING DEAD™ hasn't done much for my career. It's mostly a conversation piece for me.

But I am proud to have done something that's known all over the world. I'm proud to have invested in it, and I'm proud to have worked in it. I'm always glad to associate myself with the film. The whole experience was one of real camaraderie. It's the only film I've been involved with that the crew had fun doing. I always get a kick out of the heavy "analysis" that people use when they discuss the film after museum showings and the like. The film was mostly created by chance. We didn't plan to make it a "comment on the times" There wasn't any symbolism planned in. For example, the "explanation" for the zombies' existence was my suggestion, about halfway through the film. But it's very self-satisfying to know you've set a trend."

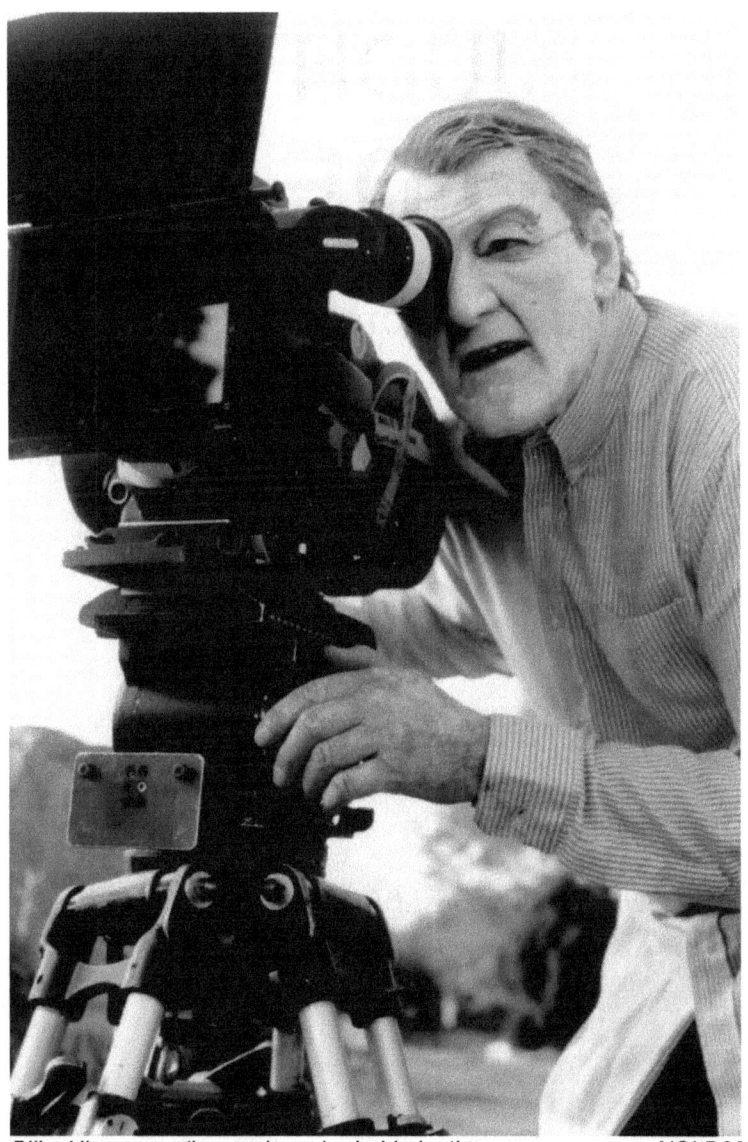

Bill Hinzman (in make-up) behind the camera on NOLD30
(Photo by Bob Michelucci)

JUDITH O'DEA

ACTOR

INTERVIEW BY PHIL FASSO

April 2013

NIGHT OF THE LIVING DEAD™ (1968)
"BARBARA"

© Image Ten, Inc.

To describe Judith O'Dea as a classy, eloquent lady just isn't adequate. Judith's been answering questions about NIGHT OF THE LIVING DEAD™ and George Romero for 45 years now, but when I interviewed her this past Friday night at Chiller, her joy made it seem like it was her first time. She took interest in just how much I loved the movie, and why. The interview came across as if we were old friends having a lovely chat. That makes it unique.

How did you get involved NIGHT OF THE LIVING DEAD™?

Well you've heard the adage who you know? Well, it really makes a difference. I had done musical theater and all kinds of television and radio commercial work. I worked for Karl Hardman at his studio Hardman Associates in Pittsburgh. Karl played Harry Cooper in the movie. I had gone off to Hollywood to become a star out there and within a year I got a call from Karl saying "why don't you come on home and audition for a film that we are making?" So I left Hollywood, came home, auditioned and got into the film.

Getting that part truly changed my life.

What is it like being part of a classic film?

To say it's a thrill doesn't quite capture it. It is something that every single day of my life... I am amazed, I'm awed and I'm really honored to have been fortunate enough to be a part of it.

What was George Romero like to work with?

George was wonderful. He's a very intense fellow and one of the most creative fellows that I know. He is also one of the most real. He's a down to earth guy. He knew what he wanted with every single shot. I could tell he had it all in his head and he would explain "this is what we're going for and this is the physical action" and then he gave us the freedom to bring it to life which for an actor is a wonderful thing not to be micromanaged, but to be given that freedom. He did that.

Tell us a little bit about Duane Jones. What was it like working with Duane?

He was wonderful. He was a very intelligent fellow. He was always reading and, if he wasn't on set, he was smoking a cigarette to be honest with you and reading some more. I thoroughly enjoyed our working together. With the hitting scene, it had originally been written for me to hit him three times but he wasn't comfortable with that so he talked with George and said he'd rather do it this way... "She hits me and then I hit her." And that's the way it was done.

What about Barbara? She seems to get a bad rap.

You mean because she doesn't say a lot? Well you stop and think if you just saw your brother being killed and then you've seen the dead come back to life ... then you tried to explain it to yourself? I think Barbara's reaction is very true and believable. She had to pull from within in order to survive. I understand in the 1990s when NIGHT OF THE LIVING DEAD™ was remade she survives carrying an Uzi because by then women were standing up saying "hey don't mess with us anymore we've got good heads *and* good bodies." So I think they're both appropriate in their own way. But I truly respect my Barbara for the way she handled it

How do you feel about doing the convention circuit and meeting with fans?

To have the joy to talk to people who have supported the film, who have really made it what it is today, is a great pleasure for me. It has given me a greater respect for those people who embrace horror films than I've ever had in my life. It is a unique group of people and some of the nicest that I have ever met.

Judy signing a photo at a recent convention

RUDY RICCI

FEBRUARY 14, 1940 – MARCH 8, 2012

ACTOR, WRITER, INVESTOR

INTERVIEW EXCERPT FROM
***QUESTAR* MAGAZINE**
OCTOBER 1980

NIGHT OF THE LIVING DEAD™ (1968)

© Image Ten, Inc.

"The group of us that became The Latent Image started making movies together in college. NIGHT was our first attempt to make a few bucks so we could keep making feature films. I think now that if we had known the odds against our success when we started, we would have thought twice about trying. But it came out of our love for making films. That, of course, left us as babes in the woods. Our filmmaking abilities were plentiful, but we came up short on the con man and accountant skills you need to be successful in films. All in all, NIGHT was a pleasant surprise and nearly everyone in the original group is still active in the business."

VINCE
SURVINSKI

JANUARY 25, 1912 – MAY 7, 2001

ACTOR, INVESTOR

INTERVIEW EXCERPT FROM
QUESTAR MAGAZINE
OCTOBER 1980

NIGHT OF THE LIVING DEAD™ (1968)
"POSSE MEMBER"

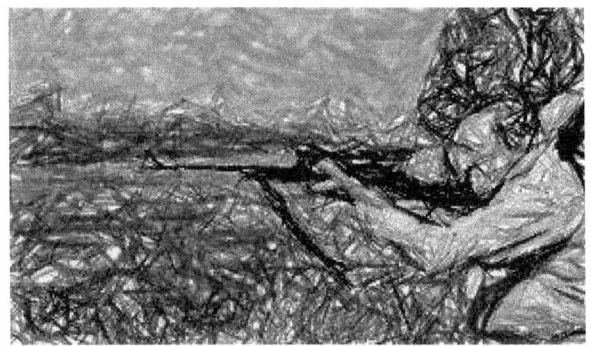
©Image Ten, Inc.

Well, I realized my childhood ambition to be a "movie actor". But that was squelched when I went to a kiddies' matinee to see the film. When the scene came where I shot the hero, those kids' reactions scared the hell out of me. I stayed in the theatre until it was cleared, then made a hasty exit and headed for a nearby alley. I think those kids would have pelted me with half-eaten candy bars, gooey popcorn, soda pop and whatever.

When you are involved in every aspect of filmmaking, from the planning stages, preproduction, filming and post-production, you experience a feeling of accomplishment when viewing the finished product.

Now we have a large staff, all specialists in their fields, and I feel like the low man on the totem pole. There is no film credit for my current job: "keeper of the johns." But I love it.

"NIGHT OF THE LIVING DEAD"

"NIGHT OF ANUBIS"

Budget Breakdown

AN IMAGE TEN PRODUCTION

THE LATENT IMAGE, INC.
247 FORT PITT BLVD.
PITTSBURGH, PA. 15222

1. PRE-PRODUCTION:
   A. Casting
   B. Story
   C. Screenplay (scripting)
   D. Location Search
   E. Make-up Testing
   F. Talent Contracts
   G. Production Design
   H. Legal Fees

   TOTAL $14,000.00

2. ACTORS FEES:
   A. Principles
   B. Extras

   TOTAL $20,000.00

3. PRODUCTION:
   A. Location fees
   B. Sets
   C. Set Furnishings
   D. Equipment Rentals
   E. Crew
   F. Film Stock
   G. Music
   H. Editing
   I. Sound Effects
   J. Lab Work and Finishing
   K. Titles and Special Effects

   TOTAL $60,000.00

4. ARTWORK AND ADVERTISING:
   A. Pre-sale Exploitation
   B. Miscellaneous Artwork and Ad lay-outs

   TOTAL $20,000.00

   BUDGET TOTAL $114,000.00

PREPARED FOR IMAGE TEN, INC. BY
RUSSELL W. STREINER - VICE PRESIDENT
VINCENT D. SURVINSKI - TREASURER

Pay PITTSBURGH NATIONAL BANK
PITTSBURGH, PA., OR ORDER
VINCENT D. SURVINSKI
46-4-782875

NIGHT OF THE LIVING DEAD™ budget break down; NIGHT OF THE LIVING DEAD™ was almost titled "Night of Anubis"
(Photo courtesy Laura Parker)

REGIS
SURVINSKI

DECEMBER 2, 1928 – NOVEMBER 2, 2012

INVESTOR

NIGHT OF THE LIVING DEAD™ (1968)

Although Regis has passed away, I am able to offer our readers several images that have been provided to me for publication from Mr. Survinski's daughter Laura Parker.

Regis Survinski with two pictures of the truck explosion. The mannequin is not visible in the movie. (Photo courtesy Laura Parker)

Russ Streiner and George Romero are on the far side of the car. Judith O'Dea is inside. Vince Survinski is kneeling at the side of the car and John Russo standing to the left. Possibly Gary Streiner is leaning in with the light meter, or it could be Joe Unitas since he was in charge of lighting.
(Photo courtesy Laura Parker © Image Ten, Inc.))

Rege Survinski's original NOTLD stock certificate. It is stock number 4, shares 2, dated 1st day of May, AD 1967
(Photo courtesy Laura Parker)

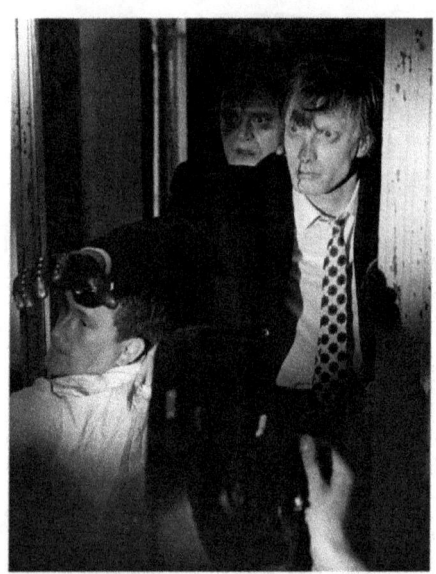

Johnny making entry into the farm house. Regis Survinski is lower left. In the foreground is George Romero's hand holding the camera.
(Photo courtesy Laura Parker © Image Ten, Inc.)

L to R: Bill Mogush, Paula Richards, Regis Survinski and Jack Givens.
(Photo courtesy Laura Parker © Image Ten, Inc.)

KYRA SCHON

ACTOR

PERSONAL REFLECTIONS

NIGHT OF THE LIVING DEAD™ (1968)
"KAREN COOPER"

© Image Ten, Inc.

Early one morning in 1967 my mom woke me up with the words, "Honey, you're gonna flip." When I groggily asked her why, she replied, "You're going to be in a movie!" I was never particularly easy to rouse for school, but that morning I shot awake and I felt like the luckiest kid on earth.

My good fortune was due to the fact that my dad, Karl Hardman, was to be a co-producer of NIGHT OF THE LIVING DEAD™ (not its working title). He would also play Harry Cooper, the film's cellar-obsessed control freak, and they needed a kid to play his daughter. I just happened to be the right age, in the right place, at the right time. By age nine, I had spent hundreds of hours soaking up every horror and sci-fi movie on Pittsburgh's *Chiller Theater*. (The host of that show, Bill "Chilly Billy" Cardille, would also capture a role in NOTLD, as himself.) Being a little monster in a horror movie was something I had never even dared to dream, but I couldn't imagine anything better.

Despite the vast span of time since 1967, I've managed to retain some specific memories because I've continuously talked about them over the course of the last four-plus decades. Hearing other cast members' recollections has occasionally jogged my memory, as well. Mostly, I remember being fascinated by the proceedings.

Kyra and Bill Hinzman together again

Working with my dad was the best part, of course. He let me hang around watching him when I wasn't needed, and I enjoyed observing various aspects of the production. He applied my very minimal makeup (a small bone of contention for me - I really wanted a gooey-looking wound like some of the other ghouls) and directed me in my few short scenes. The "trowel scene" was the one I remember most clearly, and it's obviously the one that has garnered the most attention over the years. He had me stabbing into a pillow - a stand-in for Marilyn Eastman. When I asked him how many times he wanted me to stab the poor pillow, he just said "just keep going." I guess it seemed like overkill to me at the time. When directing me in the scene where I attacked Duane Jones's character Ben in the living room, my dad said he wanted me to limp a little bit. I asked him, "Why am I limping when I was bitten on the arm?" I thought that was pretty sound logic for a kid. He did not agree.

© Image Ten, Inc.

I enjoyed watching my dad working with the other actors. I was not particularly comfortable being the center of attention, so when I could blend into the background and watch the others doing their scenes, it was enthralling. I remember being present for the scene when my dad's character Harry Cooper was shot and stumbled down the stairs into the basement. The trouble was that in take after take, he kept getting tangled up in the coat tree at the top of the stairs, and it followed him out of the room. Everyone was laughing so hard they were in tears. When I finally saw the finished film, despite seeing my dad shot and killed onscreen, remembering the reality of that scene always made me laugh.

Having been a part of NIGHT OF THE LIVING DEAD™ was an enormous blessing in my life, and one that continues to unfold. So many people in my life would not be there if not for my involvement in the movie. I've met some of my dearest friends through horror conventions and other venues related to either NIGHT OF THE LIVING DEAD™ or the horror genre in general. I am grateful for the supportive network of horror-loving friends I have in my home town and throughout the world. And I am eternally grateful to all the members of Image Ten for allowing me to participate in their project.

Kyra with Karl Hardman and Marilyn Eastman

GEORGE KOSANA

ACTOR

PERSONAL REFLECTIONS

NIGHT OF THE LIVING DEAD™ (1968)
"SHERIFF CONAN V. McCLELLAND"

© Image Ten, Inc.

George Kosana, in addition to his duties as Production Manager, starred as Sheriff McLelland in the horror classic, NIGHT OF THE LIVING DEAD™, and delivered his famous ad-lib line, "They're dead! They're all messed up!"

He played an abortionist's front man in George Romero's follow-up movie, THE AFFAIR, which was a romantic comedy. He continued his acting career with roles in THE BOOBY HATCH, THE DEVIL AND SAM SILVERSTEIN, and three other independent films. In December 2012 he acted in his eighth film. That project is not yet finished, and not yet titled.

Still active in the entertainment business, he delights his many fans when he appears at horror conventions for autograph signings throughout the United States. In setting up his table at conventions he often reflects; "It seems The NIGHT OF THE LIVING DEAD™ has just completed filming. Then the convention doors open and reality confronts him.

He allows fans to prepare him for question and answer sessions he is to partake in, but audience questions directed at panel members reflect his willingness to share his experiences in front of, and behind the camera."

Bob Michelucci asked, "How do you prepare yourself for Question and Answer sessions at conventions and participate as a member of the panel?" I thought that over for some time until it donned on me. "You Don't."

The answer to that question can be found in experience and history. Not *what year was this discovered*? Or *who/was the first to sail...*?, but in my own work history, involvement in various films, and working on projects. I attribute my approach, and attitude toward work, to my service of four years active duty in The Marine Corps back in the early fifties. You have a job to do, GET IT DONE.

I am George Kosana; the Production Manager on, and played The Sheriff in, George A. Romero's, original, 1968, black and white release; The NIGHT OF THE LIVING DEAD™. To help you better understand my genesis and evolvement in the entertainment business we must begin at the beginning. My initial exposure to film, and the entertainment industry, begins in Pittsburgh, Pennsylvania.

In 1960 George A. Romero and Russell W. Streiner form The Latent Image Studios, a commercial production house designed to produce television commercials, travelogues, documentaries, and other types of films.

The creative and expressive potential this genre offers is immediately apparent to me, and, when an entry level position is offered in 1961, I don't hesitate to take it. 13 years pass quickly.

My education in the film industry expands. I learn production from behind the camera, the intricacies involved in script preparation, the importance of attention to minute details, continuity, running times, and camera moves necessary in producing advertising, television commercials,' promotional films, infomercials, working long hours, most important, raising the budget, and a host of other duties.

It's build a set one day, the next day, set up tripod, camera, string cable, arrange lighting, run film stock out to the lab, act when, and in whatever, I'm called upon to appear in. What is really amazing, every once in a while, were even paid. Every person working there, regardless of position, shares the common goal, "let's make full length feature films."

Over time, money is saved, and finally there is enough to buy a good camera. At last we have the equipment we need, the crew, we know what needs to be done, how to do it, and the collective "we" agree. "Let's make a movie." George Romero and John Russo write the script. Along with outside investors, we invest our own money, and finance the film.

While George, Russ, Jack, myself and others audition actors for various roles, Richard Ricci, Rudy Riccis' cousin, says" I look like a cop." It's unanimous, "I am Sheriff Conan V. McClelland in the film."

While studio business must continue, fitting locations are found, the farmhouse in Evans City Pennsylvania and the Evans City Cemetery.

In what spare time I have, I study my script, memorize the dialogue, and form an insight that helps create a "feel" for the character. This translates into," Who is this character", what personality traits does he have?" Is he a red neck, or sophisticated? "What area does he reside in?" "Is he in a position of responsibility", authority", "How does he handle or react to pressure in the situation he must deal with?" "What about his wardrobe?" and so on.

When required to participate in "Question and Answer" sessions I address questions directed to me, and recall-what I was involved in during that part of the film, and how does it pertain to the question. I answer as honestly as my ability to remember allows me, and 1never lose sight of the fact that the question is important to the person who asks it. My answer must always be thorough and accurate as possible. I hope I can still recall scenes I did forty-five years ago.

As Russ Streiner says, and I borrow from him, "We made a movie; the fans made that movie a success. The fans don't owe us, we owe the fans." I never lose sight of that fact.

In closing, and without running the risk of bragging, I must mention other involvements.

I have acted in eight films to date, my last in December of 2012. I have also been offered a part in a ninth picture. I have been interviewed for it, and when funded, will act in it.

I am also a writer. My full-length feature, A-run, situation comedy/screenplay, WE'LL TRY AGAIN © won the Silver Award in international competition for best screenplay comedy at The Houston International Film Festival, The Festival Of The Americas.

Under the cover of MADNESS, TIMES THREE © I have written a trilogy that deals with three distinctly different psychological disorders.

My short story, *Tiffany's; It's Get Even Time* ©, is published by Burning Bulb Publications, and is available in their anthology from *The Big Book of Bizzaro*.

On the back burner, and when I find the time to do it, I have acquired All World Rights to write a true story about an unsolved murder.

In addition to that, I am an award-winning photographer, and long term active member of The Photographic Society of America where I have won ribbons, a medal, and several acceptances. Our affiliate organization The Washington Camera Club awarded me Photographer Of The Year for my photograph of "Sunset at Marshal Point Lighthouse in Maine."

At the beginning of this article I mention GET IT DONE. Allow me to explain how this attitude, and approach, shapes Conan V. McLelland, The Sheriff, in NIGHT OF THE LIVING DEAD™.

As that character I am forced to confront a horrible, dangerous crisis. Protect and serve the public is the sworn duty of all law enforcement, but, how to accomplish it when up against an army of crazed ghouls who seek, attack, destroy, and devour, living humans? How, or why, they exist is not a consideration. My mission, and objective, is to save humanity. My only option; destroy them all.

Put the problem in perspective. No one wants to fight, but when forced to kill or be killed, why not fight to win? It's an ugly, dirty, job, but one that absolutely must be done. Flavor everything with a no-nonsense, red neck, persona, dressed in a suit, armed with a high-powered rifle, a bandolier of ammunition, and hopefully, a believable Sheriff emerges. Not every situation was all work. Some things were funny.

The Evans City house was plumbed for, but had no, running water. The entire crew took turns in a bucket brigade. We would walk to the creek behind the house, fill empty buckets with water, carry those to the upstairs bathroom, and fill the reservoir tank so the commode could be used. Two or three full buckets always sat nearby in case they were needed. And we took turns sleeping in that house.

One night someone slipped up. They let the word get out. We intended to shoot the scene where the truck is blown up at 2:00 in the morning so the noise wouldn't alarm the population of Evans City. Rege

Survinski and Tony Pantanella made the explosive charges around 1:30 a.m.

We pushed the broken truck into position down the road well away from the farm house. We couldn't help but notice most of the population of Evans City had gathered on both sides of the road and sat in lawn chairs, patiently awaiting the big event. We had to enact crowd control and move them safely out of the blast range.

The truck was filmed as it exploded around 3:00 a.m. When it finally did go boom the entire population cheered for some twenty minutes.

Another important consideration was the cellar in the house. It wasn't dug out or finished. A person of average height couldn't stand upright and walk around. They'd hit their head on the rafters and beams. We recreated that cellar in the basement of The Latent Image Studios in downtown Pittsburgh and shot all the cellar sequences there.

We travel to Washington, D.C. to film the scientists and the Army General as they are bombarded by questions from news reporters who seek answers to explain what is happening. With the White House as a backdrop their questions go unanswered. Two separate incidents thoroughly amuse me.

The Lincoln Town Car had to have a General's License plate on the front bumper. In the middle of a parking area designated for high ranking military officers we stripped off the actual plate and attached the General's plate. No one questioned us.

The second occurs around noon when the actor who is to play the General must change from street clothes into his uniform. We have no dressing room, or facilities, so, in the middle of a Washington street we hold blankets up, form a circle, put him inside, and in our make shift dressing room, he changes clothes and gets into costume.

What is hard to believe but is true. No one questioned us, what we were doing, or asked to see our permits.

Making movies does have its moments.

NIGHT OF THE LIVING DEAD
40th Anniversary 1968 – 2008
© 1968 Image Ten, Inc.

GEORGE KOSANA
(aka – Sheriff)

NIGHT OF THE LIVING DEAD™ press kit
(© Image Ten, Inc.)

(Photo courtesy George Kosana)

RUSS STREINER

ACTOR, INVESTOR

INTERVIEW BY PHIL FASSO

Death Ensemble

NIGHT OF THE LIVING DEAD™ (1968)
"JOHNNY"

© Image Ten, Inc.

It's safe to say that without the efforts of Russ Streiner, NIGHT OF THE LIVING DEAD™ would have been a different film. His onscreen presence as Johnny sets the tone for the film straight out, and his finesse as a producer helped to get the picture made and sold, and in turn, in front of audiences. He's also a genuinely nice guy, who was generous enough to spend some time on the phone with me for an interview. During the course of our conversation, we discuss working with George Romero, his acting turn as Johnny, and casting Duane Jones. He's got some great perspective on the film, and was happy to share

How did you first get involved with George Romero?

I started off wanting to be an actor, which I pursued through high school. And after high school, I went to the Pittsburgh Playhouse School of the Theatre, for acting lessons. While I was there, I was working in stage shows at night, and at one of those, I was cast with another fellow. His name was Rudy Ricci, and we shared a dressing room. Rudy had been attending classes at Carnegie Mellon University) back then it was called Carnegie Tech). He was taking art classes there, and he met George Romero in class. George was transplanted, from the Bronx to Pittsburgh, to go to Carnegie Tech's School of Painting and Design. Rudy brought George over to one of our shows one night, and that's how I first got to meet him. Then, within maybe six or eight months, George called me and asked me if I would be willing to be an actor in a movie that he was putting together, called EXPOSTULATIONS. And I told him I would. I showed up for my very first day of production, and really became intrigued with the whole film production part of the business, which I knew nothing about. I stuck with EXPOSTULATIONS as an actor, and then also helped out on the crew. That's how George and I first met. And we worked together for a while after that.

How did your experience in commercials and industrial films help you to put together a feature film?

Any time you get a chance to practice your craft, whether it's in short form like TV commercials or longer form like industrials, all of that goes to help you refine your craft. And that's certainly how our whole group got helped out, all of which led up to 1967, when we did the actual filming of NOLD.

What was the genesis of NIGHT OF THE LIVING DEAD™?

Basically it started off when we first got together. We always knew that we eventually wanted to do a feature film. So during the early '60s, by doing TV commercials and industrial films and educational films, we were able to accumulate equipment—by the time NOLD came around in 1967, we were actually a self-contained unit; we had everything we needed: camera equipment, sound equipment, studio facilities, mixing equipment, editing equipment, lighting equipment. Then all we needed was a script. And in late '66/early '67, John Russo, who was working with us, and George Romero started to put together the beginnings of a script. We all chipped in ideas. And that's how it got started.

What things did you bring to your role of Johnny?

Well, first of all, my body. Secondly, I got the part of Johnny almost by default. We had put together all of our pre-production efforts. We had most of our casting done, but we didn't have Johnny. And the cemetery scene, coincidentally, was the very first scene we filmed, and we didn't get finished with all of the filming that day, so we had to relegate it to a second day of filming. As it turned out, it was also the very last day of filming we had, so it was kind of an unusual circumstance. But when it came to the first day of shooting, we still didn't have a Johnny. And the group said, "Well why don't you just do Johnny?" And so that's how I got it. So I'd like to say that it was some tough auditioning competition, but it was nothing like that. I just happened to be around, had dark, horn rimmed glasses, and got the part.

When I got the part, I decided that I wanted to give him a couple of unique characteristics. One of the things was how he taunted and tormented Barbra. I wanted to make sure that he was always on the edge with Barbra, complaining about the time of day and how early they had to get up, one thing after another.

And one of the wardrobe elements, of course, were the driving gloves. I wanted to make a big deal out of the driving gloves, which were my idea, because I knew when Johnny came back at the end of the film, I wanted to give him some sort of wardrobe signature that the audience would instantly know that it was him. It would be nighttime, his glasses were gone, he would be surrounded by these other dead things. So, I wanted to give him a really instantaneously signature, and that turned out to be the driving gloves. And it was a device that really worked.

Johnny seems like a very annoyed character? What's your view of him?

Well, I think underneath it typifies the kind of sibling relationship that a lot of brothers and sisters have. Brothers especially get into taunting and tormenting their younger sisters. And I think that comes through to the fans, and a lot of people comment on it, "Oh, that's how my brother used to treat me," and so forth. So I wanted to keep it realistic on that level. That plus the fact that we as actors knew what was coming, we knew that this was going to be the very first onset of the living dead things, and I just wanted to set the stage for the gloomy things to come.

A great part of the subtext of NOLD is about family. Johnny and Barbra don't get along, and the Coopers argue as their daughter is dying. Family was also behind the camera for you. How was it working with your brother Gary and your mother?

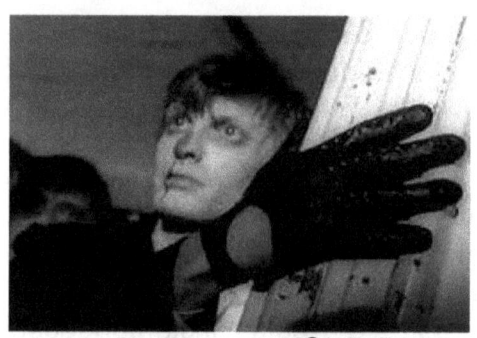
© Image Ten, Inc.

Well, obviously, it was a very good experience for all of us. My brother Gary worked with George Romero and myself since he was in high school. When we filmed NIGHT OF THE LIVING DEAD™, Gary was 21. So he had been working with us for a few years and was pretty good at any number of tasks. On NIGHT OF THE LIVING DEAD™ in particular, he did an awful lot of the location audio work, and then ultimately the sound mixing work.

And as far as my mother, you have to understand, the way we were constructed at that time. The company that George and I started was called the Latent Image. And everybody's family—George's family, my family-- became an extension of the Latent Image. So when it came to filming NIGHT OF THE LIVING DEAD™, we recruited my mother, my aunt Norma and several other family members to be zombies and so forth. And my mother provided one of the key props for the cemetery sequence, her car. So, all around, it was pretty much of a family effort.

And of course there was the fortuitous car crash that George worked into the film

Well it wasn't so much fortuitous for my mother. As I said earlier, the cemetery sequence was the first scene that we filmed, and it was also the last scene. Now, we filmed NOLD in 30 days, but we had a break in the middle so we could go back and do regular commercial work that was keeping groceries on the table. But from the time we filmed the opening scene until we got around to the time we finished the closing scene, my mother was driving her car back and forth to work, and someone crashed into her car. And I said, "Don't get it fixed, because we need a way to stop the car when Judith O'Dea releases the handbrake in the cemetery to get away from Bill Hinzman (the film's cemetery ghoul), and we'll do something with it, we'll crash it against a tree or something like that," and that's what we ended up doing. We filmed it in a way to make it look as though the car actually crashed into the tree. So we were very resourceful. We had to take all the negatives and turn them to positives somehow.

What was George Romero like as a director?

Working with George was always a good experience. But understand, we had a business that we started in 1961, when we incorporated it. So George and I had been living together, literally like brothers, sharing apartments, sharing literally everything. We were as close as or closer than brothers for quite a few years heading up to NOLD. And it was always great working with him. And I hope he feels the same way about working with me.

Casting a black man in the lead was a bold move, whether intentional or not. What statement do

you think it made, having Duane Jones in the lead?

Well, it became more of a statement than we had originally intended. Quite simply, Duane Jones was the best person to audition for the part of Ben. Up until we met Duane, our friend that I mentioned earlier, Rudy Ricci was supposed to play the character of Ben. The character was originally supposed to be a rough truck driver. A mutual friend of George's and mine was a woman by the name of Betty Ellen Haughey. She grew up in Pittsburgh, but at that time she was living in New York, and she knew of Duane Jones. He'd started off in a suburb just outside of Pittsburgh, yet he was off in New York making a living as a teacher and an actor. And she said to us, when NIGHT OF THE LIVING DEAD™ was really developing in the preproduction and building steam, "You should really meet this friend of mine from New York, his name is Duane Jones." Duane happened to be in Pittsburgh visiting his family for one of the holidays, and we auditioned him. And immediately, everyone including Rudy Ricci said, "Hey, this is the guy that should be Ben."

So that's how we cast him, and we knew that there would be probably a bit of controversy, just from the fact that an African American man and a white woman are holed up in a farmhouse, being attacked by these living dead things outside, and they don't really know what it's all about. So we thought there might be some element of controversy, but that it was worth going through that controversy to have Duane Jones as the lead.

When did you realize that NIGHT had become a classic? And how did that feel?

Well, we knew almost right away that it was going to be a popular film. Classic is something that developed over the years. We set out to make the best, scariest movie we could, with the relatively small amount of money that we had. The fans made it a classic. And of course, any time that happens to any type of work, it is incredibly flattering.

One of the notorious issues with NIGHT is the copyright issue. You're still fighting to get the copyright restored. Do you think this will ever be resolved?

I hope it will be. But it is an issue. The copyright was wrongfully taken from us in the first place by the Copyright Office. And so it's a battle that won't end, and is going on to this day. We never, ever, ever intended for that picture to be offered up into the public domain. And this dispute has been going on with the Copyright Office ever since. Curiously, since NIGHT OF THE LIVING DEAD™, they've changed the copyright laws so the same kind of thing could not happen to a picture today. So that's the underpinning as to why we believe that our position is ultimately right. And we just have to keep pursuing it, because it is rightfully our property, and there's no other argument to be made. It's our property.

You make many appearances at conventions. What appeals to you about the convention circuit?

The key thing would have to be coming face-to-face with fans, and understanding that this is a property that is now 41 years old, and it is quite phenomenal. It doesn't happen to a whole lot of movies that 41 years after the fact, the fans are showing up, they still want to meet you, still want to shake your hand, get an autograph. And that is most flattering. I can't say that I understand it, but I certainly do appreciate it.

Your appearing at your brother Gary's Living Dead Festival next week. What are you looking forward to with that?

Well, it's the same kind of thing, except the Evans City Living Dead Festival has a separate, special ingredient in that Evans City is the hometown of NIGHT OF THE LVIVING DEAD™. Practically all of the film was filmed in and around Evans City. (The only exceptions were all of the basements scenes in the film; they were filmed in the basement of our office building in downtown Pittsburgh. And then we'd set off one weekend to go to Washington, D.C. to shoot the sequence with the reporters and scientists and so forth). Aside from that, everything else was filmed in Evans City. It is truly the hometown of NOLD.

© Image Ten, Inc.

Russ with Bob Michelucci, John Russo and Bill Hinzman
(Photo courtesy Bob Michelucci)

NOTLD has become a cultural phenomenon that has lasted more than 40 years. As you prepare to meet fans at the LDF, what are your reflections on the film now?

Well, NIGHT OF THE LIVING DEAD™ has taken on a life of its own, so to speak. How that happened is, new audiences are constantly being introduced to it. And that has perpetuated this film, and apparently, enough people think it's a good picture, they find different things they like about it. But this common creative effort that we all put together as a team, people are still sensing that there's something good and valuable in the story itself. And so, coming up to the Annual Living Dead Festival in Evans City is another opportunity to meet fans. But these fans are even a little more special, because they make the trek in from wherever they are into Evans City to celebrate the film where it was made. And that's a really good feeling for any creative endeavor.

GARY STREINER

SOUND ENGINEER, INVESTOR

INTERVIEW BY PHIL FASSO

Death Ensemble

NIGHT OF THE LIVING DEAD™ (1968)

© Image Ten, Inc.

Among those names made famous by NIGHT OF THE LIVING DEAD™ some 41 years ago, Gary Streiner might not be the first to come to mind for the film's many fans. Though Gary was not as prominent as George Romero or Gary's own brother Russ, he was part of a tight-knit team that produced what would become not only a classic horror film, but a classic film in general. One of the ten original investors in NIGHT, his role as the film's recording guy and sound mixer gave him an inside view of the movie. He was kind enough recently to discuss some of his experiences on NOLD with me, as well as his second annual Living Dead Festival, an autograph signing and showing of the movie which included many first time guests, including Judith Ridley. www.thelivingdeadfest.com

How did you first get involved with George Romero?

I got involved with George Romero through my brother Russ, who was studying to be an actor at the Pittsburgh Playhouse. George came there one night to see a performance that my brother was in, brought there by a mutual friend.

So George and Russ became friends and later partners, off doing their thing. I was still in high school, not really working full time at all, and they were off doing a project called EXPOSTULATIONS, a 16 mm film that George was in the process of making. So I came out one Sunday or Saturday, to be part of a crowd. They had a quasi-company going, called The Latent Image, and at that point in time, they were just doing still photos, and nuts and bolts for industrial catalogues, I mean the most mundane stuff you can possibly imagine. They rented a place over on the South Side of Pittsburgh, and George was living there; it was a great space, because it had 3 sections to it: the front space the office. And I'm like a 15-year-old kid at this time, and this is all like playing/work. You go off to brother's quasi-office, you know.

George was a chronic soda drinker, and he just couldn't speak in the morning without a cigarette and a Mountain Dew. So there were three sections to this building, the front was the office, and the middle section was used as a studio and it was literally filled with Mountain Dew bottles. Because George was a chain smoker, he put all of his cigarettes out in the bottles. So my first professional job was to get all the cigarette butts out of the pop bottles, so I could then take them up the street and return them for the 3 cent deposit, for my paycheck. To kind of get an idea of how many pop bottles there were. There were weeks when I made $50.

What was the development process like on NIGHT OF THE LIVING DEAD™?

Define "development process." (Laughs) What area? The concept of it or in the overall of it?

How much were you involved in the back story, before the actual filming started?

Again, I was the kid, so I got to sit on the floor a lot and listen to these guys sort of thrash all this stuff out, George and Jack Russo and my brother and Rudy Ricci and sometimes Richard Ricci, in those brainstorming sessions. And we were also running a company, so I had other chores and duties to do, but the hardcore script development went on mostly after I went home. You know, it was really a fun time, in contrast to most of today's occupations. Even though none of us was making much money, 99% of the time, we would've chosen to be there than be home. That really made it fun, because the times that we were there were always exploratory. There weren't a lot of meetings posted on schedules, that kind of thing. The forum was extremely open, there were never like closed door meetings, they were all conference room chit chats rather than, "Okay, it's 9:30 and I'd better be in Board Room B for the latest script revisions." It was much more organic, much more, "Well, we're tired with what we're doing over here, " then we'd go have our meetings in a big conference room on the 5th floor. It was carpeted, and there was a couch, and you know we could just sort of lounge around and meet.

And so that's where most of the screenplay developed. My involvement was limited, because I just truly couldn't keep up with the big boys intellectually, I guess. And that's really the way I felt during that time. I was like in awe of these guys, and I was so proud to be able to physically, and ultimately intellectually, able to help facilitate a lot of the things. I was another strong, strapping young man that lugged gear around and really helped to execute other people's ideas.

NOLD was somewhat of a family affair, with Russ and your mom involved. How was it working with family?

During NIGHT it was totally comfortable, it was great. Working with family, you knew the enemy; you knew where the skeletons were buried. There was the overshadowing thing that I will always feel, the younger brother syndrome. It's not that it put me in a position of discomfort, by any means; it was just a fact, that I was the younger brother, and 6 years less cultured. George had been Fine Arts major at Carnegie-Mellon, so he at least understood the concept of creativity, and again, I would say that my brother understood the creative aspects of the business a lot more. He had been in much more creative endeavors. But as a 15-year-old kid, I hadn't created any of those categories in my personality as of yet.

Some people give their all for art. You nearly gave your life. Can you share that story?

(Laughs) Well, that's a bit of an exaggeration. Our level of expertise was limited, and our level of naiveté was enormous. We didn't know a lot. It was just like, "Okay, this chair was on fire a few minutes ago, I'll check it out, make sure there's no sparks. Then I'll take this plastic gallon jug of gasoline and dump it all over it and light it again." It was not very bright and not hugely safety cautious, by any means. So yeah, I did in fact catch myself on fire, and it was pretty terrifying, and considering everything, yes, I am hugely lucky. I had a full gallon of gasoline in my hand, which was now being flung in the air and all over me, all up my arm. And it could've hit my face, anything could've happened. And thank Bill Hinzman (who played the Cemetery Ghoul), he probably was a volunteer fireman somewhere, he knew to tackle me to the ground and roll me on the ground. The whole thing was over in like 30 seconds.

What was George Romero like as a director?

Well, I think George by his own admission didn't want to be the director. The last thing he wanted to do was have to be the boss. That was not something that he did naturally. Later as I became a more accomplished producer working with many different directors, I learned that it's the producers challenge to, surround the director with as many creative people possible. But at that time in Pittsburgh those people didn't exist, so a lot more fell on George's shoulders. I don't think the film that came out would've been the same if George wasn't the person he was or at the professional level he was. And that's a compliment, because he wasn't a film director at the point; he'd never directed anything over 60 seconds prior to that. He did a few other longer format films, maybe 10 minutes long, travelogues and things like that for Pennsylvania, but never had to carry dialogue, or carry a scene for a long period of time.

So sometimes he took a lot longer to figure it out, like a lot of young directors I've worked with since then. They never know whether it's really right or wrong until they see it. They end up doing things a bunch more times than they have to, just to have the ability to see it more times and figure it out. So I think George fell into that category as much as any real first time director would.

I think that one of George's biggest asset is his creative mind, his ability to think mental pictures and conceptually, I think that's what a fine artist does before he puts a brush to a canvas or a sketch pad. He could develop a creative idea, certainly as he went on, George could see things artistically, which the rest of us didn't necessarily have the ability to do.

When did you realize that NIGHT had become a classic? And how did that feel?

I really felt it for the first real time last year. You can't live a life and go pretty much anywhere in the world that somebody doesn't know about it, your signature as a film, "Gary Streiner, he was one of the people who made NIGHT OF THE LIVING DEAD™." It's pretty amazing, the various companies I've been in at times, to think that some pretty high-powered tables could be brought to a halt by the mention of NIGHT

OF THE LIVING DEAD™. I would get spikes like that all through my life.

And then last year when I decided to do the first Living Dead Festival. I hadn't even been in Pittsburgh in 20 years, so it'd been a long time. Meeting fans last year, I just started thinking,

"Wow, this is a real thing, this isn't just something like a blip, this happened in my life," 40 years later, it's still going on, and you have humans out there just so many people I've met over the last year who really care about this film. The last year made me realize, not necessarily that the film was a classic, but what being a classic meant, and that's a much bigger rush than the actual making of the film.

Romero continued to make *Dead* movies after NIGHT. Have you seen these other films?

I'm going to be very honest with you. I'm not a big horror fan. It's like one of the last things I would put on my list. I just happen to be a guy who made a film, and that same film happened to become real popular. You know, I've seen... I couldn't even tell you which ones I've seen. I've seen THE CRAZIES, DAWN, DAY and LAND. But it's not like I was the guy hanging on the edge of the whatever, waiting for the next drop.

One of the notorious issues with Night is the copyright issue. Your brother Russ is still fighting to get the copyright restored. Do you think this will ever be resolved?

I doubt it. I have to say, just for the pure ownership aspect of it, it would be nice, to get it restored, just for the historical accuracy of it. Certainly, our potential to capitalize on the project that we actually created is more difficult. But I'm finding that none of that really matters. Everyone knows who made NIGHT OF THE LIVING DEAD™. We can't change it, it was a stupid mistake; I can't be sure at how many levels the mistake was made. Obviously, it was made on more than one level. We were a bunch of naive kids, and we didn't know all things we necessarily should've known. Now if Russ were here with me, he might have a whole different point of view. Which is why he and Jack, in particular, they're the primary trustees of Image Ten (NOLD's production company), so they would. But I'm sure it'll be an ongoing project with Russ until he dies, to get it restored, at any opportunity possible.

After 40 years, NIGHT OF THE LIVING DEAD™ finally got the documentary it deserved in Chris Roe's ONE FOR THE FIRE, in which you participated. What are your thoughts on that documentary?

I will be flat out honest in saying, when I saw it, I said, "Well, it's not an embarrassment." Did I think it was certainly the definitive documentary of this film, or the makers of this film? No. I don't think so at all. I think it was a lot of passion, and a lot of labor that went into finding people and then interviewing them. But I know I said more pertinent things than what actually got used in the film, and I think that just about anybody who was interviewed for the film could say the same.

I did a film called COMEDIAN with Jerry Seinfeld, where we had 600 hours of material, and it took pretty close to 16 months to cut that into a film; and I don't think ONE FOR THE FIRE got that type of consideration.

Romero and a number of the others involved in NIGHT did the convention circuit with the 40th Anniversary NIGHT OF THE LIVING DEAD™ Tour. You didn't take part in that. Was that because of the Living Dead Fest?

No, I wasn't asked. Certainly, Jack and Russ and Kyra Schon and Judy O'Dea, and to some degree Karl Hardman and Marilyn Eastman and George had been doing conventions for a lot longer than last year. I think it just became a convenience, and a salable commodity to say, "All right, this is the group of people that have been out there doing it. We'll just commission them." The eight people that travelled became a neat little bundle. I went to the Chiller show, this April, mainly because I just wanted to go and say hello to a lot of people that I've met online and also to meet a lot of people like you that are helping get the festival off the ground. Now, with the Living Dead Festival, I have the ability to have my own event, that I can partake in here in Evans City, and it's not going to get any better anywhere else.

You're now gearing up for the 2nd annual LDF. How did the Festival come about in the first place?

A guy named Rick Reifenstein was on the Evans City Historical Commission, and they were sitting around, having one of their meetings, saying, "What can they do to raise funds?" So, one of the projects, or one of the things that got added to the list was the 40th anniversary of the NOLD coming up, "Maybe we can do something." Rick had that idea, and then contacted me, I guess it was a year ago last February, and said they were thinking about doing it, would I be interested. My circumstance was certainly open to it, and that's how it all began. Rick and I started yammering ideas, and we spent most of the year—creatively thinking of what we could do. And then we got down around August, and said, "How are we gonna pay for this?" And that could've been the end of it right there.

But finally, I just said, "Look. We have a couple of opportunities, they won't cost us anything; we can be part of the Oktoberfest parade, that's free; we can be part of the Evans City Halloween parade, that's free; and then we can have a screening at EDCO Park." And that's really what happened. And it was just such a magical little screening. We had literally put out about 4,000 flyers, and probably did that no more than 3 weeks before the event. And we got 300 people to show up for the screening.

NOLD fans have been calling for Judith Ridley to do conventions for years, and this year's Living Dead Fest. How did you convince her to come?

I had to put a roof on my brother's garage. It wasn't about negotiations, it wasn't about money. Russ has been talking to Judy for years about, "You really ought to think about coming out and doing one of these shows. The fans would love to see you. It would be financially rewarding." And she just really didn't care to do it. This wasn't part of her life; she certainly does not perceive herself as her role in the movie. A little like me, she went on and had a life and did other things. Judy is actually having a hard time understanding why anyone would show up to see her. That's a reality. And that's just the sweet, brilliant innocence of this whole thing.

Well, Russ and their two kids Rachael and Justin had been harping on her for a long time. And so they finally wore her down; she finally responded positively, to the notion of doing a show. I was standing in his driveway, replacing a roof on his garage, and I just looked at him and said, "Do you know what this would mean, if she were to do our festival first?"

Judy is really happy that she can do her first show in the comforts of the family. It's not like she has to go out and thrust herself into some 35,000+ fans. This'll be a real nice way for her to enter into it. And I'm hoping it'll be really great for the fans, because I think they'll have an opportunity to get more quality time with her, and in the end, that's all people really want. They don't care about vendors tables.

NIGHT OF THE LIVING DEAD™ has become a cultural phenomenon that has lasted more than forty years. As you prepare to meet fans, what are your reflections on the film now?

Paul McCartney was just on the Letterman show a couple of weeks ago. And Letterman asked him some question like "How long before you came on The Ed Sullivan Show were you guys big?" And Paul McCartney just stared at him with this blank stare and said, "Two days." He proceeded to say, 'It's kind of crazy, but the details of most of those years are a blur to me; you get a much better answer to those kinds of questions from the fans." And I found that to be absolutely true. I really want to meet them, the people who have given so much of their life to this film, and I guess I want to fulfill their expectations in whatever way I can. My perceptions tell me that's accessibility right now. That's the thing that the true hardcore fans want more than T-shirts or posters or vinyl stickers. They just want to be able to meet and greet the people and have access to the people who made the film. Last year, there was a doctor who came up and introduced himself at the screening, who had his 12-year-old son with him, and he introduced his son. And he said, "Thank you so much for putting this event on, because my son has never seen the movie, and now I can properly pass on the heritage, through this official screening." That nearly brings tears to your eyes because it's so real and so sincere.

I don't profess to be anything more than the guy who recorded the sound for the film, and one of the original 10 investors, who now, through a quirky set of circumstances finds himself in the driver's position to carve out the definitive NOLD festival. 300 people came out to see this film on a freezing cold night in October in a park. And all of them went away saying "thank you." When does that happen in America?

CHARLES
CRAIG

ACTOR

INTERVIEW BY PHIL FASSO

Death Ensemble

NIGHT OF THE LIVING DEAD™ (1968)
"ANNOUNCER"

©Image Ten, Inc.

What was your role with Hardman Associates before you came to work on NOLD?

I went to Hardman on staff as a writer and an actor. I came to them out of WCKY Cincinnati, my previous radio job, where I had been doing radio and news primarily for many years. My job at Hardman was to create radio commercials for the advertising agencies. So that's how I happened to be on premises.

How did you get involved with the film?

I was in my office one day, and Karl Hardman came in. I knew there was a film underway; at least I was more or less aware of it. And he came in and filled me in on the concept of the movie, and what was causing all the strange circumstances, premised by the movie. And asked if I, as a newsman, could create what might be simulated news reports of the events going on. That was right down my alley, so I changed the paper in my typewriter and went to work.

So you wrote those parts then.

Yes.

You play a radio broadcaster in the film, and later you show up on television newscasts. How do you think the use of the news enhances the film?

My hope was that it would add a note of verisimilitude, believability to the whole concept. That was how I intended to present the news reports as they were coming into the news desk, to give it a sense of immediacy, a sense of, "Hey, this could really be happening."

Not only did you play a broadcaster, but you also played a ghoul. How did that come about?

I was on location out in Evans City, out in the farmhouse. I went up initially out of curiosity. Of course, the Hardman folks were up there too, so as long as I was there, I was not about to get out of there without getting into makeup. So I did.

Did you prefer playing the broadcaster, or the voiceless ghoul?

The ghouls had very little to offer by way of voices. So I think probably the most important contribution I made was as the newscaster.

Were you surprised by the success of NOLD?

Well, yes, I was. I had no idea of the audience response to this. As a matter of fact, it was quite some time after it premiered in 1968 that I became aware of crowds were showing up for it.

And I thought, "Well, this took me by surprise." Very, very pleasantly.

You contributed to the documentary AUTOPSY OF THE DEAD. How did it feel to take part in that?

That was a nostalgic trip for me, because I did my part of it in the former Hardman studios building, which has been totally remodeled since we were there. But I can visualize the way it was when we were there, on Smithfield Street. It was pleasant to be able to hearken back to those creative days. I think where they filmed me, at one time; we were in what I could characterize as a rehearsal hall. We were doing quite a lot of work in industrial films, live industrial shows. And so we would rehearse music and our dance steps and our choreography and our moves in this rehearsal hall, which is now a series of partitioned offices.

You've recently hit the convention circuit with others from NOLD. What appeals to you about conventions?

I think it's marvelous! I was not yet on the start of the convention circuit. It became apparent to me by happenstance. A friend of mine from New Jersey, Jim Cironella, let me know about it. And I said, "Yes, I'd love to be part of that," so I did, starting in the early part of last year. It's amazing to see the turnout of people who really, seriously enjoy the film, and to become aware of many of the things that viewers are reading into the story I know George Romero has often said, "We didn't set out to say that at all." But some people are reading into it some sociological implications. And fine, that's good. It wasn't meant to be that way. It wasn't put there for that purpose, but it turns out that's probably one of the things that contribute to the life of the movie.

NOLD has become a cultural phenomenon that has lasted more than 40 years. As you prepare to meet fans at the LDF, what are your reflections on the film now?

As I say tongue-in-cheek, the movie is just like our ghouls; it refuses to die. It will go on, I think because it has definitely become a classic, and the timing of its release and its storyline was happenstance and happily so, because at that time, in 1968, the public was very much aware of space adventures. The Russian Sputnik had been launched just a short time prior to that, and people were really interested in outer space, and what are these things bringing back to Earth. So you had the premise of what's causing our ghouls to come back to life.

And your voice will continue to be part of the legacy as the film goes on for many more generations to watch.

Well, thank you. I am very, very fortunate to have been on the scene when the film was getting off the ground, and I just count my lucky stars that I was there to be able to work with this fine group of people. Really not only good folks, but talented folks and they will always be cherished in my memory.

JOHN A. RUSSO

ACTOR, SCREENWRITER, INVESTOR

INTERVIEW EXCERPTS FROM
QUESTAR MAGAZINE
OCTOBER 1980

ICONNSOFFRIGHT.COM
MAY 2008

NIGHT OF THE LIVING DEAD™ (1968)

© Image Ten, Inc.

INTERVIEW EXCERPT FROM
***QUESTAR* MAGAZINE, OCTOBER 1980:**

This film turned out to be very important for everyone who worked on it. It was well respected and well known, so it became a door-opener for us. We've been able to get financing for other projects just because of our NIGHT OF THE LIVING DEAD™ experience.

At first, it wasn't that case. The talent and effort we demonstrated was initially written off as a fluke. With

George Romero's success, the "fluke" mentally seems to be gone.

We earned credibility through the industry that a film, a good film, could be made in Pittsburgh. We opened up filmmaking for Pittsburgh, and now there are many more Hollywood productions here.

We no longer get those "crazy bunch of kids" stares. For me personally, it has been very good. I have been able to publish four books, and have three more contracted for, with films maybe coming from them.

© Image Ten, Inc.

NIGHT OF THE LIVING DEAD™ was the first step off the ground for all of us. It was a big risk. But we took the chance...and it paid off.

John Russo confers with Bill Hinzman on the set.
(Photo by Bob Michelucci)

"MESSING WITH" NIGHT OF THE LIVING DEAD

At long last I am going to respond to the misinformed people, the so-called critics and the plain nut cases who have railed against my writing and direction of 18 minutes of new scenes in the 30TH ANNIVERSARY EDITION of NIGHT OF THE LIVING DEAD™.

The folks who think that only George Romero has the right to "mess with" our movie are badly mistaken. To begin with, I was the one who came up with the idea that the "attackers" in our story should be dead people; and that they should be after human flesh. Without those two key ideas, you don't have NIGHT OF THE LIVING DEAD™ (NOLD). And you probably don't have the "Zombie Genre" as we know it today -- the genre that has launched the careers of so many famous filmmakers and has thrilled so many dedicated fans.

So if anybody should get credit for inventing the so-called "modern flesh-eating zombie," I have as much claim to that as anybody does. George and I very much collaborated on the screenplay. I re-wrote his first half of the story, putting it into screenplay form and doing considerable re-writing, and then I went on to write the second half of the finished screenplay. Many other important ideas, in addition to the idea of the attackers being recently dead people and flesh-eaters, were mine alone, such as the killing off of our hero, Ben, by the sheriff and his deputy. Also, the way the escape attempt unfolded, the way Harry turned on Ben, etc., etc.

By the way, just to make myself perfectly clear, none of my comments here are meant to disparage the excellent work done by George Romero. Without George, the movie would not have existed. And we were solidly behind him as director. But we were all young and this was our first feature movie. We didn't know as much then as we know now. So some of the mistakes I have talked about in this article are mistakes we would not have made later in our careers.

To backtrack a little, the way that the 30TH ANNIVERSARY EDITION came about was that Russ Streiner and I, who are the trustees of the corporation that made NOLD, got word that a certain distributor was going to make their own version -- with their own new scenes added. We have a fiduciary obligation to Image Ten, Inc., and its shareholders to make as much money for them as we can, and to prevent others from stealing or profiting from our original work.

So we accepted a deal from Anchor Bay to make a 30TH ANNIVERSARY EDITION with new scenes added, and they paid us $200,000 to do so. Again, we are obligated not to turn down these kinds of deals, because we and our shareholders have been ripped off enough over the years, to the tune of millions and millions of dollars.

Another very important motivating aspect of the Anchor Bay deal was that we used the vast majority of the money they paid us to totally remaster and refurbish our original negative, employing the processes that were state-of-the-art at that time. And the original movie -- without any editorial changes -- was released along with the new edition, so that all fans of the original got to see and purchase NIGHT OF THE LIVING DEAD looking better than it had ever before looked on video.

I immediately phoned George Romero and asked if he would go along with the deal. He said that he would and that he and I would do the writing together, as we had before, and that he would direct, as before. But he got tied down with another project, and I ended up writing and directing.

Anchor Bay loved the final result. The head buyer, Jay Douglas, called me up and said, "You've done something that very few filmmakers have managed to accomplish. George Lucas did it with STAR WARS and now you've done it with NIGHT OF THE LIVING DEAD™. I've been a life-long fan of your movie and I can't tell where the old scenes and the new ones begin and end; it's seamless! A beautiful job!"

Russo giving some direction to zombie girls for one of the new insert scenes being shot for NIGHT OF THE LIVING DEAD's 30th Anniversary Edition
(Photo by Bob Michelucci)

Now some of the "zealots" who rail against what I've done think that NOLD is so "pure" that altering it is like altering the Mona Lisa. But NIGHT OF THE LIVING DEAD™ was never a pristine work of art. It is full of bad edits, bad screen direction, continuity blunders and bad acting. It rose above its faults because of the powerful story and zealous hard work of a small group of talented people, including not just George Romero and me, but Karl Hardman, Marilyn Eastman, Judith O'Dea, Duane Jones, Gary Streiner, Russ Streiner, Bill Hinzman, George Kosana, Vince and Rege Survinski -- plus our numerous shareholders and friends, too numerous to mention.

In conceiving of the 30TH ANNIVERSARY EDITION, I

wrote a PROLOGUE and an EPILOGUE -- because adding material front and back is the surest way not to mess too much with the original. I also added a couple of scenes to the interior. In doing so, I wanted to have some fun addressing some concerns that we worried about 30 years earlier but did not have enough money to take care of them. For instance, we wondered if audiences would buy that this farmhouse in the middle of nowhere could be surrounded by a slew of ghouls. Where had they all come from? So I wrote in a couple of scenes and characters, illustrating that many of the ghouls could have come from the "Beekman's Diner" that Ben talks about at length while he's tearing apart the dining-room table.

We also did some pretty nice "tweaking" in spots, during editing. For instance, we fixed the famous "jump cut" in the basement; this was Bill Hinzman's idea, and we fixed it even though we thought 30 years ago that there was no way to do so; but Bill came up with a way, and we implemented it. Also, we fixed the mistake when Ben is disposing of the mutilated body in the upstairs hallway; in the original cut, you can see the face of the live girl "doubling" as the mutilated body (it was actually Kyra wrapped up in the carpet); but we fixed this by cutting into the shot a bit later.

So, in making our 30TH ANNIVERSARY EDITION and earning a substantial amount of money for our shareholders, we had a great deal of fun "messing with" our movie, and we were cognizant of what Stephen King said when an interviewer asked him what he thought of what Hollywood had done to his books. He said, "They haven't done anything to them. There they are, right there on that shelf."

NIGHT OF THE LIVING DEAD™ in its original form, the form that has stunned, scared and entertained millions of people over the years, is still intact in all its "classic glory." So, lighten up, folks! The 30TH ANNIVERSARY EDITION is just another "fun venture" that can be talked about, argued over, and appreciated or not appreciated in its own way. And you ought to be glad anytime our poor, hardworking, ripped off shareholders get at least a small chunk of the millions and millions of dollars that have ended up, over the years, in the pockets of con men, thieves, rip off artists and disreputable distributors.

INTERVIEW EXCERPT FROM ICONSOFFRIGHT.COM, MAY 2008

How is it that you became interested in writing and creating film?

I became interested in writing probably from around the time I was in fourth grade. A substitute teacher asked us to each write a poem, and when she came to my desk and read my poem, she accused me of copying it from one of my school books. She spent the rest of the afternoon searching through my books trying to find the poem I had "copied" which of course she did not find because my poem was wholly original. So I discovered early that I apparently had a talent for writing, and I also loved to read. I got acquainted with and loved Mark Twain's writing when I was in fourth grade, too.

Like most people, I loved going to the movies but I didn't think I'd have that kind of career because I thought all movies were made in Hollywood. But when I met George Romero and Russ Streiner when we were all 18 years old, through George especially the idea of actually making movies on our own began to excite me very much. Still, my main goal up to this time was to become a published novelist -- and I eventually succeeded at that, and to date I have had fifteen novels published worldwide, plus four nonfiction books dealing with movie making.

And how is it that you all met?

I met George Romero when he came to Pittsburgh at age 18 to attend Carnegie Tech, which is now Carnegie-Mellon University. I was 18 also and was enrolled at West Virginia University -- an English Education major. George was in the fine arts program and during his first day on campus he met my close friend Rudy Ricci and Rudy mailed me a letter saying he had met this great guy, very wild and talented, who instead of drawing the nude models in "life" class, would spend his time drawing scenes from movies. So when I came home for Christmas vacation, Rudy and I drove to George's apartment in Pittsburgh, and he came out dressed like one of his favorite characters in VIVA ZAPATA -- he was wearing a sombrero, carrying pistolas, and wearing a drooping black mustachio. We went to a Dairy Queen and the girl slammed the window shut and wouldn't take our orders.

Later, also through Rudy, who later became one of our original investors in NIGHT OF THE LIVING DEAD™, I was introduced to Russ Streiner, who was acting in a play. We all became fast friends, and after some failed attempts at making a movie comedy, as Russ and George were forming a little company called The Latent Image to make commercials and try to raise money to eventually do another feature film, I got drafted into the Army. I dreamed of joining Russ and George when my hitch was up, and that's what happened. We all worked our butts off, learned the film business from scratch, won lots of awards eventually, and built up our assets and equipment to the point where we could launch our first feature -- and that became NIGHT OF THE LIVING DEAD™.

What kind of horror do you remember growing up with?

I grew up reading EC comics like TALES FROM THE CRYPT and true crime stuff, etc. I also saw all the movies that came into town, including the horror movies like FRANKENSTEIN, DRACULA, THE WOLF MAN and so on. I went to see all the "B" horror movies Hollywood was cranking out and was almost always disappointed. They all had the same hackneyed plot -- a giant grasshopper or a giant caterpillar would menace the world, it would kill the town drunk, the scientists would eventually figure out what was happening, and the National Guard would come in at the end and destroy the creature with flamethrowers.

Yeah, that pretty much sums it up (Laughs). What inspires you to frighten?

I always yearned to see a good horror film and did not see too many until I saw INVASION OF THE BODY SNATCHERS, PSYCHO and FORBIDDEN PLANET

(which was technically science fiction, not horror, but I consider it to be horror in a way because it did have "monsters from the id" which was a very horrific concept.)

When we were developing the concept for NIGHT OF THE LIVING DEAD™ I told everyone that we needed to make a movie as stunning, shocking and scary as INVASION OF THE BODY SNATCHERS.

One of my favorite themes is how the best intentions of scientists, political leaders, religious figures, etc., often can go awry -- through lack of understanding, greed, selfishness, lust for power, and any other sort of human failing. So therefore my novels and movies strive to be cautionary tales with strong themes and realistic characters.

Your contributions to the film world, especially the horror genre, have become cult classics! Your most popular works have been NIGHT OF THE LIVING DEAD™ and RETURN OF THE LIVING DEAD, which was based off of a book you wrote. But now you have a new film project called ESCAPE OF THE LIVING DEAD, starring Tony Todd and Kristina Klebe. Can you tell me a bit about this film and how you're transferring it from graphic novel to the screen?

ESCAPE OF THE LIVING DEAD was a screenplay before it was a comic book. William Christensen, president of Avatar, liked the script and offered to adapt it into comic book form. The fans loved the result, and we made the Top Ten of horror comics nationally, and it spawned T-shirts, sweatshirts, shot glasses mugs, etc. To date I have written or collaborated with Mike Wolfer and William

Christensen on ten sequels, all contained in a huge graphic novel after first debuting as multi-part comic books. The first graphic novel of ESCAPE OF THE LIVING DEAD, based on my original screenplay, sold out. And so, when you have that kind of terrific fan response to a story, then the movie really deserves to be made and needs to be made.

The screenplay itself has never been turned down by anybody including all the actors, actresses, agents, publishers, producers, financiers, etc., who have read it -- this must be some kind of record in the movie business. ESCAPE has a very strong heroine whom I like to think of as "the Sigourney Weaver" of horror films. The character's name is Sally Brinkman, and she is to be played by Amber Stevens, a beautiful and talented young actress who stars in the ABC/Family Channel series, GREEK. Sally's father, Henry, is being played by another terrific actor, Tony Todd. They are both in great jeopardy in the movie and must try to save each other from a dire fate. We (producers Sam Sherman, Joe Majestic, Dave Mendez and Russ Streiner, plus myself as writer/director) are very, very pleased to have Kristina Klebe and Gunnar Hansen as part of a wonderful cast in this movie. The story is not a trite carbon copy of things that have been done before, but instead has elements I have never seen in any other zombie movie, and I think this is why the readers of the comic book versions are so in love with what we are doing.

When can we expect to see it in theatres or on DVD?

As I write this (May 10, 2008) one of our producers on ESCAPE OF THE LIVING DEAD, Joe Majestic is on his way to the Cannes Film Festival to secure financing for the project. We anticipate shooting later this year, probably by October, so editing won't be complete until sometime in 2009 when the picture will probably be released theatrically.

When you wrote RETURN OF THE LIVING DEAD, it wasn't as humorous as they portrayed it in the final movie. How did you feel about the film when it was released and how did you feel about Tom Savini's NIGHT OF THE LIVING DEAD™ remake?

The original screenplay for RETURN OF THE LIVING DEAD was written by me, Russ Streiner and Rudy Ricci, and was stark horror in the vein of the original NIGHT OF THE LIVING DEAD™. But, when we sold the property to Fox Films, it was then sold to Orion, and they decided that "straight horror is dead" -- which in my opinion is always a fallacy -- and they hired Dan O'Bannon to add the comedic elements and to direct the result. I thought Dan did a marvelous job, and I liked the movie. Dan and I got along superbly well, and he very much liked my novelization of his script.

Russ Streiner, George Romero and I co-produced the NIGHT OF THE LIVING DEAD™ remake, and George as executive producer tapped Tom Savini to direct. It was Tom's first stint as director of a theatrical feature, and he did a decent job -- but overall the picture did not turn out as well as we hoped. This was not all Tom's fault. There were other factors beyond our control, having to do with the distributor, the tornado-like weather, and so on.

Personally I loved Savini's version and I have yet

to meet another horror fan that feels any different. Savini himself even said at Texas Frightmare that when it was initially completed he didn't like it, but watched it more recently and decided it was actually a really good movie. Tornado-like weather!? Do you have any real life horror stories from being on set during the bad weather?

Even though I mentioned tornado-like weather, nobody got killed or anything. We were on the fringes of the tornados which meant that we and all our costumes, makeup, equipment, actors and staff were getting drenched and the intended big wrap-up of the remake couldn't happen very effectively.

I kept coming up with ideas for things that could be done pretty well on short notice, and I'd run the ideas past George and he'd say, "Let's do it!" For instance I suggested that one of the zombies should eat a mouse, so I went into the special effects quarters and asked them if they could make one, and they said, "Sure!" Then I got them to rig a zombie who died from an overdose and with the needle still hanging out of his arm, and they did that, too. And so on -- anything to dress up the movie even though the circumstances were trying.

How did the "40th Anniversary world tour of NIGHT" go? How many conventions had you attended for the event?

The 40th Anniversary NIGHT OF THE LIVING DEAD™ Tour was a wonderful experience. It is always great to meet the fans and keep in tune with their likes and dislikes and remain on the same wavelength, so we can continue our careers on a high level and keep on pleasing the fans in a big way. As I said, our intention from the beginning has always been to really pay off the fans who buy the tickets. They are often disappointed by movies that fall short of their expectations, and we never want to be the filmmakers who fall short. On the tour we went to Pittsburgh, Dallas, Los Angeles, Baltimore, St. Louis, Phoenix, Orlando, etc. We also made appearances at Sitges in Spain, London, Portugal, Germany, Belgium and Italy.

I understand you have also written a handful of books on the subject of film making and screen writing. These books are even revered as "bibles" to those in the industry. What kind of tips do you give to film-makers?

It is true that my filmmaking books are considered "bibles of the industry" and I am very gratified by this. I was originally a teacher, and I still teach with Russ Streiner in the Master Mentoring Program that is an integral part of our movie making course at the DuBois Business College in DuBois, Pa. Many filmmakers, both beginners and noted filmmakers as well, give me credit for jump-starting their careers. For instance, when I met Quentin Tarantino at the LAND OF THE DEAD premiere, he said that he made a movie that he did not complete, and then he read my books, took notes and made charts, and that is what guided him through the making of his first complete movie.

That's amazing! Giving advice to one of the most influential filmmakers of our time!

The advice I give aspiring filmmakers is really too involved to cover in the space of an interview - that's why it takes an 18-month course to scratch the surface. I can say that the goal of our program is to bring the students to a professional level as rapidly and smoothly as possible, and we are meeting that goal.

They learn how to do everything from TV commercials to industrial films, documentaries, sales films, etc. -- all the way up to feature film production, marketing, and working out contracts -- the entire business side as well as the creative side of filmmaking. What we give them -- because of our long and comprehensive experience in the business -- cannot be learned so readily and so comprehensively anywhere else in the country. The Master Mentoring Program that Russ Streiner and I implement is entirely unique and quite fruitful in terms of its ability to inspire and educate young filmmakers on a high plane of accomplishment.

Can you tell me a bit of what it's like to be in your classroom? What are your teaching methods?

Our Movie Making Program at DuBois Business College, about a hundred miles north of Pittsburgh, takes place on a beautiful campus where total student enrollment is about 250 students overall. But the Movie Making Program is very personal and hands-on. Everyone gets a great deal of personal attention, and right now our first class their numbers seven students. We have on-campus apartments available, and we also have federal aid for qualifying students, a terrific staff, and so on.

What are some of your favorite films, not necessarily horror but films of all genres?

I love all sorts of films, not just horror. Some of the best horror films, in my opinion, are PSYCHO, ALIEN, HALLOWEEN, INVASION OF THE BODY SNATCHERS (original version), plus the original DRACULA, FRANKENSTEIN and WOLF MAN movies. I also liked THE HOWLING. A list of my favorites would include SINCE YOU WENT AWAY, THE BEST YEARS OF OUR LIVES, VIVA ZAPATA, GLADIATOR, STAR WARS, GOODFELLAS, THE GODFATHER, PULP FICTION, RESERVOIR DOGS...I could go on and on.

How do you feel about the horror today and how it has changed with time?

Today's horror films are sometimes too dependent on shock and gore instead of good plot, theme and character development. Also I'm not a big fan of the over use of CGI effects. There is always room for a movie that does have fresh ideas, and good plot, theme and character development. Also, good casting is extremely important. For the most part, people go to the movies to see and identify with people, not lavish effects.

John, Bill, and Russ on the set of NOLD30
(Photo by Bob Michelucci)

RICHARD CATIZONE

ANIMATOR, ACTOR

PERSONAL REFLECTIONS

NIGHT OF THE LIVING DEAD™ (1968)
DAWN OF THE DEAD (1978)

(Photo courtesy Rick Catizone)

I've had the good fortune to work on quite a few George Romero films. This was an outgrowth of working together on some commercials and other projects. We eventually moved into the same building. Bob Wolcott, original owner of The Animators, was approached by The Latent Image to produce the end visual sequence and the titles for NIGHT OF THE LIVING DEAD™. I was doing about 90% of the animation photography at that time. George decided he wanted to handle the end of the film with camera moves on still photographs. The only way to accurately do camera moves on small stills, maintain focus, and most importantly, end up at exactly the desired composition was to do them on an animation stand, animated a frame at a time. So, Bob and George sat down and George explained what he wanted. Crops were drawn on acetate or tracing paper overlays for the camera crops. I then worked out the camera positions, and then the camera moves. That was before computers, and so involved my working out a fair amount of math to divide up distances moved in all five direction (N,S,E,W, and Zoom) to end properly. It also meant using a little algebra to also calculate slow in and slow out, so the transition wouldn't jar anyone. Bob also worked out some of the moves when I would be on lunch break, to save time. George's design has a stark effect, and an appropriate one, for as the hero's life ends tragically and shockingly (especially at that time, because it was so unexpected) everyone else who IS still alive is frozen in these stills. It's really a very poetic statement when you think about it.

Still from NIGHT's end credits © Image Ten, Inc.

I also recall at one point Jack or George mentioning that they were changing the name to NIGHT OF ANUBIS. I said they better check that, because I had seen that title in an issue of Famous Monsters of Filmland magazine. Actually, probably a good thing, because the NIGHT OF THE LIVING DEAD™ title is so unique, and we see what it spawned. I was never one of the on-screen "living dead", but I WAS one of the voices for the zombies in DAWN OF THE DEAD. One day Mike Gornick came down to our floor and said he needed "zombie voices". I think there were about five of us from The Animators, a couple from the architect firm above us, and George and Christine (Forrest) and others from The Latent Image. At first it was a little odd, but everyone quickly got into it. They wanted active zombies, passive zombies, mad zombies, attacking zombies, etc. So, as we all lowered our voices into guttural mumblings we got pretty good at it I thought. Of course, at some point inevitably we all would just crack up because it was also just so funny. I think George may have even laughed first one of those times. I mean, you really have to picture it. Everyone was trying to "look" a bit zombie-esque to make it easier as we made these zombie growls. I think Mike may also have asked us to also do some milling around, so the voices would change placement and relative volumes. Inevitably you would look at a co-worker or a boss or George and just crack up when you realized what we were actually doing.

While almost my entire career has been behind-the-camera, as an animator and special effects artist, I actually did step in front of the camera in the original version of THE CRAZIES. There was to be fight scene, and Bill Hinzman knew I had been studying jiu-jitsu and karate for about eight years at that time. He asked me if I'd like to stage a fight scene with some martial techniques, and be the soldier who gets beat up... and I said, "Sure." So I worked out a little routine, worked with actor rehearsing it for about half an hour. The most dangerous part was that, for part of it, I designed a move for him to parry my punch and do an arm break. I explained that I was allowing myself to be in an extremely vulnerable position and was relying completely on his being absolutely accurate and not going too far. Mainly, I just said that I know things can get carried-away in the heat of an action, but he needed to focus on that moment for my safety. I wasn't worried about taking the kicks and the rest of it. Thankfully, he was very sensitive, and it went off without a broken arm. The sequence was also designed to be a continuous set of moves, finishing off the soldier in a very short time. It feels a little awkward to me when I watch it, because the plot called for picking up some other story point, but when we get back the fight isn't over, it's still finishing up from the last move. Now, Bill also said that since I was the one taking the beating, I might as well just finish the shot. I said, "Fine." I later found out that meant that I get my mask ripped off and slapped around a bit. It was interesting as the actor said that he was going to be a little rough with me and he would be into the scene. Now, I was SUPPOSED to be kind of out-of-it as he "questioned" me. Try as I did, I just could not completely hold back my training, and you will see my hands slightly deflecting his slapping me. I was holding back, not reversing the situation and finishing him off, as much of my training was in ground-fighting. Actually, the hardest thing was that in the cool night air, our masks fogged up a lot from our warm breath. That also made it a bit complicated seeing what we needed to do in the fight, but everybody was having issues at some point I guess. That was my sole screen appearance. I had a great time working on all the films with George and the rest of The Latent Image gang.

Rick Catizone and Mike Gornick at a recent con holding a CREEPSHOW 2 cell (Photo courtesy Rick Catizone)

PART TWO

DAWN
OF THE
DEAD

GAYLEN ROSS

ACTOR

INTERVIEW BY NEIL FAWCETT

© March 2005 by Homepage of the Dead

DAWN OF THE DEAD (1978)

© Laurel Entertainment, Inc.

I believe before DAWN OF THE DEAD you hadn't acted professionally. What were you doing prior to the film?

I was a managing editor (as I was finishing college) of a literary magazine called Antaeus' and The Echo Press', which I'm happy to say is still considered one of the finest publishers of poetry and serious fiction, as well as essays.

I started taking acting classes, caught the 'bug' and the rest was history or sort of. I did some small plays around New York, but DAWN OF THE DEAD was my first professional acting job.

How did you hear about it, and what made you go for the role?

My very good friend, Sarah Venable, who played a housewife in MARTIN, knew that they were casting the lead female of DAWN, and looking for a blonde. She shrieked at me in my acting class and said "you're blonde!!" I had no idea what she meant until she connected it with the film, and that I should audition.

When you read the script, what were your initial reactions?

I had no idea who George was (I never saw NIGHT OF THE LIVING DEAD™) but thought the script was very literate, especially for a horror film. And my standards were pretty high, coming off reading poetry for several years.

With a lot of bloody and ghoulish scenes and much of the shooting taking place through the night - at times in cold conditions - did you ever wonder what you had got yourself into? Did you wonder if you chose the right project for your debut appearance?

I was just very happy to have a job; my panic came from realizing I was the lead female and this wasn't a rehearsal. My first time looking at dailies I was in such a shock at my acting on screen, I crawled back into my hotel room for several days. Luckily, they didn't need me for filming. I saw all sorts of twitches and blinks, and I knew I had to get focused. There was a break between filming for a month, and I took the script to a very famous Russian acting coach, Mira Rostova (she was Montgomery Clift's coach.) She took it all very seriously, and it was quite funny as she was instructing me through the scenes with zombies, after I explained what a zombie in fact was.

Do you have any particular memories from working with Romero or on the film itself?

Other than being hyper critical of myself, all my memories were good. Working nights in the mall was rough as well as some of the outdoor scenes, fighting cold weather and strange sleep patterns. But all in all, it was a great experience.

Do you have a favorite scene from the film?

I think the makeup scene. I thought it was Frannie's 'moment' away from the guys, total fantasy, where she wasn't worried about survival or fighting for her place among the men.

When George got into the edit room and the movie was running long, he wanted to cut the scene - I had completely forgotten this, but George reminded me that I wrote him a two page letter defending its need to remain, and I guess he was convinced, because the scene stayed.

I believe you were involved in the casting on DAY OF THE DEAD (with Christine Forrest Romero). How did that happen? What was the experience like?

I was in New York and Chris asked if I and another good friend and the wonderful actor Bill McNulty would help cast the film. The script was quite different, much larger landscape and many more characters. Kind of a DAWN OF THE DEAD' meets BLADE RUNNER. I still remember many of the characters, they were so well written... spider, mapmaker. Every great actor in New York came into audition and loved the film.

It was really a shame and terribly disappointing that that film didn't get funded and the smaller budgeted film got made. The realized film was good, but there was no comparison to the film that should have been made.

Towards the end of the 80s, you made the move to the other side of the camera to direct a documentary (OUT OF SOLIDARITY). Since then you have continued on to make a series of award winning documentaries covering such varied topics as New York diamond dealers, stock and securities fraud, Broadway stars, gambling and even Russian mail-order brides. What took you into the field of documentaries?

After CREEPSHOW, I started to become interested in directing theater, and did several projects in New York. And then an opportunity, the Polish film OUT OF SOLIDARITY arose and I collaborated with a cameraman – who since has done three films with me, and filmed the Metallica documentary, SOME KIND OF MONSTER, and PARADISE LOST and many more. I loved the idea of working on real stories and weaving my theatrical knowledge with documentary footage.

Can you maybe explain briefly what starts one of these projects?

Sometimes I'm intrigued by subject i.e. Swiss banks and the Holocaust, or peoples' lives, as the diamond dealers in DEALERS AMOND DEALERS. If I feel it is appropriate for a broadcast channel like A&E I pitch it to them, otherwise I'm on my own raising money.

Have you ever aspired to write or direct a fictional film? If so, what sort of genre or storyline would you like to do?

No, not really.

In 2004, a remake of DAWN OF THE DEAD was released in which a number of your fellow co-stars from the original made cameo appearance. Were you ever approached to also appear in it?

I was, but decided not to do it. It wasn't George's film, and I wasn't interested.

DAVID EMGE

ACTOR

A CONVERSATION WITH PHIL FASSO

DAWN OF THE DEAD (1978)
"FLYBOY"

© Laurel Entertainment, Inc.

At the time I was cooking at a restaurant in downtown New York and I walked in the front door the restaurant and sitting in a booth off to my right there were some people and I just headed back toward the kitchen and I didn't acknowledge anybody and I heard the owner's voice say David come here I want you to meet somebody and I walked up to the table where he was sitting there with two other guys and I recognize one of the guys at the table was this guy named Rudy Ritchie who I had worked with in Pittsburgh a few years prior and I said Rudy what are you doing in New York it's great to see you so why are you here. Then we talked for a while and I basically ignored the other guy and finally the owner said David set down I want you to meet somebody... He said this is George Romero.

I said how I know who you are it's nice to meet you. What are you doing here in the city? George said, "I'm here doing some casting for a new film". So I threw my hands up in the air and asked "can I audition"? He said "sure, of course you can"... and that's how I met George Romero.

I enjoyed everything about working with George Romero. He wrote a hell of a script. He was a hoot to work with. I never saw him without a smile on his face or one he wasn't laughing. He let us explore our characters. It was just a dream job all around.

Even though the schedule was between 6 PM and 6 AM in the dead of winter at least the schedule is the same every night and there was a blizzard thrown in there in the middle, by the way. That was kind of an adventure. Again at least the schedule was consistent, but we never saw the sun for a month or more.

If you really kind of looked at the script and explore my character, it is a guy who bless his heart just can't measure up to the other SWAT guys and he wants to be really really wants to but as much as he tried he's a guy that couldn't really even laid himself out of his own bathroom in the morning. But when he becomes a zombie you'll notice that the zombies follow him. So what he couldn't achieve as a human, he achieved as a zombie. And I thought that was an interesting arc for the character. Plus it was just a great hoot to play a zombie.

Tom Savini did a brilliant job with the makeup. At one point and I was teaching college in Pittsburgh one of the things that I thought was stage makeup. So the whole thing fascinated me anyway. As a kid I always loved horror movies and always looked at the newest issue of "Famous Monsters of Filmland" magazine because they always had articles about the makeup and stuff. The whole thing was just very fascinating... that whole kind of physical transformation that takes place of my character.

© Laurel Entertainment, Inc.

I love meeting the fans at the various conventions that I attend. You know you'll be sitting there and you look up and you'll see three generations of people looking at you and then you realize that, wow, you can't kill this movie with the firemen's axe! It just goes to show you what a great job George did conceiving this movie. It's pretty much a tribute to the creative talent that went into the film that he led and by all the great people from Pittsburgh with a few of us ringers thrown in there!

KEN FOREE

ACTOR

INTERVIEW BY NEIL FAWCETT

© January 1999 by Homepage of the Dead

DAWN OF THE DEAD (1978)

© Laurel Entertainment, Inc.

How and why did you get into acting? Was it a conscious decision or more by accident?

Beautiful women! <Laughs>

Was there anyone else in your family in the industry who may have inspired you?

I had a great uncle who had a show. He had four tents, different acts and he travelled throughout the south and Midwest. I would imagine if it's in my genes it came from there.

What sort of age were you when you first thought about getting into acting and what were you doing before?

Oh... well in my twenties. Before that I was doing city politics in New York.

Do you find it hard to watch yourself on the screen?

Sometimes! <Laughs> Most times you always see the worst in yourself.

Are you self-critical?

Of course, like most actors and most people.

Do you find yourself getting nervous before you perform?

Not necessarily. There's always that little nervous energy, but not anything that gets in the way. It's always the nervous energy that gets you going, but nothing more than that.

Does it get easier with time?

Oh, I don't think so. I think it changes, you adjust. It changes from project to project depending on the character and the role, film or television. Sometimes you're still going to have some butterflies, some worries.

Have you done theatre work?

I started in the theatre in New York off Broadway. I did my first TV show there, then my first film out of New York and then some more theatre off Broadway and then of course DAWN OF THE DEAD. Then I left New York.

I keep a filmography of a lot of the actors in Romero's *Dead* trilogy and you probably have the largest one on the site. What do you believe your qualities are that have allowed you to work on such a large number of projects?

Flexibility, I would imagine. That's the reason, I would think. Being a chameleon, which is what we're supposed to be and the fact that they don't know quite where to put me and they're trying to find a place for me to fit.

Ken and I reunited after thirty-five years at a recent convention. (Photo by Dee Michelucci)

All six foot five of you?

All six foot five of me, exactly! <Laughs>

Do you consider yourself lucky being able to switch and change between so many different types of roles?

I consider it a plus. Yes, absolutely!

Did you know Romero before DAWN OF THE DEAD?

No, I didn't.

How did you get involved with it then?

Let's see... I, at the time, was doing an off Broadway play at a place called the WPA Theatre in New York and one of the guys who was in the play said they were auditioning for a character that I might fit. He gave a description of the character and I said, "I may fit that!" He told me where to go and I went over and auditioned twice and got the part.

Maybe you can answer a question about the industry in general? At times there almost seem to be little "communities" of people who work on projects. You quite often see actors or technicians popping up in several films together. This seems especially true of Romero's films.

Well there is, because most of the people who do the horror genre, they're fans themselves. They're watching other films, watching other people in other roles. I think you'll find that with most directors if they like working with someone they try to bring them in. I think Clint Eastward did the same thing with several of his people. Sondra Locke was one, even though he had a relationship with her, but he had several other guys that worked with him. One guy worked with him in three or four films. In the Gauntlet he used a few friends. Most directors do it. If they're comfortable with you, they like your work, they'll use you again if you can.

Do you have any particular memories from DAWN, good or bad?

Good or bad memories? A good memory was I met Donald Rubinstein (Richard Rubinstein's brother), a good friend. Bad!

Being snowed in at the mall and we couldn't get anything in to eat one night, so it was cookies and coffee all night.

Was the shooting schedule hard?

All night! Night to morning! We had a great dedicated low-budget crew who really worked very hard for the production.

How did you find Romero to work with!

Horrible! <Laughs> No, just joking! He was wonderful. He's a laid back guy, as big as I am, a bid teddy bear of a guy and very creative and nice! He's a nice person.

You didn't think at any time while shooting the film with very gory effects going on all around you, "My God what have I got myself in to here?"

You know, when I first read the script I thought it wouldn't play the United States - it was so gory. I didn't know the censors would let it in. I thought it might play Europe, South America maybe, the Orient, something like that, but I didn't think it would open here.

Do you have any memories of working with Savini?

Not really. He was a good make up guy. He certainly is very qualified. He was very good in what he did, he did a lot of good work and I was impressed by his abilities as a makeup artist. He really put a lot of prosthetics together that were impressive to me.

When you finally saw the completed film, do you remember what your reaction was to it?

Well, I saw the director's cut in a screening room and I was quite taken by it. I still thought it wouldn't play in the United States. I thought it was far too gory for the censors to let it in.

There's a lot of talk about the alternative ending of DAWN where you and Fran commit suicide. George Romero and Tom Savini have both said that this ending was shot along with the one we now actually see in the film. Do you recall shooting this "down" ending?

As I remember I think we shot that!

Do you think you might have preferred the "down" ending?

You know, I think the up-ending, as someone has to get away. There has to be a bright side, there has to be a tomorrow and if there's not it's quite a depressing feeling, and it was quite a depressing film as it was and something had to be redeemable.

When was the last time you actually saw it?

It played on Cinemax or something like that here a couple of months ago. I didn't know it was going to be on and I was flipping through the channels and I had to watch it for a while because it was the first time it ever played on television in the United States. For some reason DAY OF THE DEAD played on one of the cable stations; so did NIGHT OF THE LIVING DEAD™, the original, which is always played of course; so did the remake, but ours never played and I never thought it would but all of a sudden there it was so I had to take a look!

Have you seen NIGHT OF THE LIVING DEAD™?

Oh yes. I actually knew Duane Jones before he shot NIGHT. When it came out I was walking down the street and I saw Duane's picture there and his name and I looked at the title and I said, "my God!" I ran to the theatre group he was in and I said, "Duane, you're all over the marquee!" And he said, "Please, I'm trying to forget it!" <Laughs> It was very strange that Duane and I knew each other and had passed through each other's lives and I turned around and did DAWN OF THE DEAD right behind him. It's a small world!

If you had to pick a favorite out of all three, which would it be?

Oh gee, that's a tough one. I like DAY; I thought it didn't get the credit it deserved. But I would imagine that I'm like every other fan, NIGHT OF THE LIVING DEAD™ the original. It's always the best because there was nothing like it. Yeah, that's my favorite.

You later worked with Romero on KNIGHTRIDERS. How did that happen?

Well, he had already cast the actors for the film and I gave him a call and he said he was doing it and I said, "Anything for me?" He said, "Well, no! But I'll write you something." So he just wrote me something.

Do you have any good or bad memories of the film?

I'll tell you what was bad. I didn't get to ride a motor cycle! <Laughs> That was bad! I met some good friends. Donald Rubinstein was on that one too. He played one of the minor parts of the troop and did some of the music score.

If you had to choose a single medium, TV, Theatre or film, which would it be?

Oh, that's a difficult one. You know, I'm partial to theatre. I made my bones in theatre and I really love the boards. There's nothing like doing it live. Nothing like feeling audiences' breathe down the back of your neck. It's wonderful.

It must be terrifying, worrying about what happens if you forget a line?

There is some trepidation, but not as much as sometimes when you're doing a TV show and it's live, cause you've got everyone there and you know if you make a flop everyone's gonna see it immediately and you've got all the technicians running around. With the stage, you go out there, you flub a line and actors will throw it back to you or you can just weave your way around it so you get through it. Don't Stop! <Laughs> so I think theatre, films second and TV third.

We've just got *Keenan and Kel* (comedy series) in the UK. I was sitting there one Saturday morning and it came on and there you were!

It sure is! An older and a fatter version, but that's me! <Laughs>

No! From what I've heard you still work out at the Gym.

I work out about five days a week.

Do you do any other activities in your spare time?

Oh sure! I coach little league, basketball, football, that sort of thing. I also do volunteer work for mentally handicapped children.

And to relax?

I read, sleep, go to one of the islands and just lay on a beach for a couple of weeks. That's relaxing! <Laughs> Doing nothing! Absolutely nothing! Not a phone call or a letter or anything else.

Is there something you can tell me about yourself that most people wouldn't know about you?

Oh gee! Well... I was an all-state basketball player,

all-city basketball player in the state of Colorado for my junior and senior years of high school before I started acting... I once met the mayor of New York and Jimmy Carter... There's nothing I could say that's really that exceptional, but it's been a life of meeting a lot of great people and I've been blessed that way. I've met some very interesting people in all walks of life!

Finally, if you had to choose some personal favorite films, what would they be?

THEY SHOOT HORSES DON'T THEY? LAWRENCE OF ARABIA, THE PRODUCERS, THE SUNSHINE BOYS, THE OMEN, ALIEN... and NIGHT OF THE LIVING DEAD.™

© Laurel Entertainment, Inc.

JOHN AMPLAS

ACTOR

PERSONAL REFLECTIONS

DAWN OF THE DEAD (1978)

© Laurel Entertainment, Inc.

I have had the distinct honor of being included as a George A. Romero actor.

Thirty-seven years ago, in 1976, I met George. I was 27. He was in the audience of a play I was doing. Afterwards we spoke, and he told me about a film script he was working on. Two months afterwards he called me and offered me the title role in MARTIN. Shooting took place over the course of September and October of that year and by Thanksgiving, MARTIN was pretty much in the can and by the following summer Martin had been released and, on its way, to becoming a cult classic. Although none of knew it at the time.

I must have done something right because I kept getting calls from George. Next up was DAWN OF THE DEAD, a big action adventure movie where the living dead became personalized with their names

© Laurel Entertainment, Inc.

and professions. I helped with casting (mostly zombies) and anything else I thought I could do, including a small acting part, just to be around and remain part of the family!

Then came KNIGHTRIDERS. It was a ten week stint during a long and beautiful summer. Although it may have been grueling for many, it was like being at summer camp for me and others.

In CREEPSHOW, I played the *Dead* Nathan Grantham, which became the Iconic image of "Father's Day" the first of five segments in the film. No, I didn't let them put maggots in my mouth. I know, I know... I will never live it down. One of the brave female P.A.'s did it! But I did everything else!!!! DAY OF THE DEAD was a much darker take on the world and the living dead now out-populated the living. It seemed very real and intense, I thought, in its mission toward survival. It was science gone wrong and unable to see the writing on the wall becoming a perfect rounding out of the Living Dead Trilogy. Oh yes, it stared the talented Lori Cardille (daughter of the famous Pittsburgh *CHILLER THEATER* horror host icon Bill Cardille), one of the very first strong women in horror!

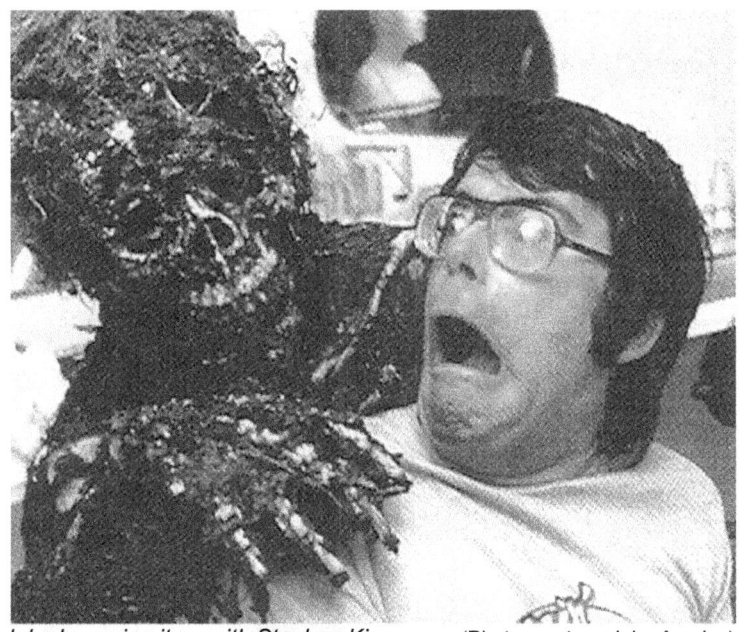

John hamming it up with Stephen King   (Photo courtesy John Amplas)

As I am writing this I can't wait until tomorrow June 22, 2013 when I get the opportunity to share, once again at the Hollywood Theater, the movie MARTIN that brought me into the Romero fold. The screening is for a great charity called Scares that Care with all of the proceeds going to people in need. It will also be my 64th Birthday.

© Laurel Entertainment, Inc.

Over the course of thirty-seven years, I have met and made hundreds of friends on a Romero film set. I have also met and continue to meet thousands of fans. I consider each and every one of them a friend. I am proud to be a Romero Actor! Thanks George!

John Amplas at a recent convention appearance

DAVID CRAWFORD

ACTOR

INTERVIEW BY
JOHN SCOTT, ERIC KENT, & LEE KARR

Conducted August 11, 2004 outside WPGH, Pittsburgh

DAWN OF THE DEAD (1978)
"DR. FOSTER"

© Laurel Entertainment, Inc.

How did you get into acting?

I've been doing it since high school. I had a teacher, who was a math teacher, but she had a double major, and the other major was in theater, and she was frustrated about that because she couldn't do it, so she would work with some of us kids.

I was always able to read easily, they'd call on me in class to read stuff out loud, and she gave me some coaching in oral interpretation. We'd read Tennyson, and Bible passages and stuff, at study hall times, and odd times, and she would coach me in how to do that. That's what got me interested.

How did you get involved with DAWN OF THE DEAD? Were you familiar with George, or any of the cast or crew members?

No, I had never met George. I went to a casting call; I don't know how I learned about it, probably in the newspaper, at their old headquarters on Fort Pitt

Boulevard downtown. And I remember Christine being there. She was helping us read.

All the local actors went down, a lot of kids from CMU, and I was a starving actor living above a pizza shop at that time. I and some of my buddies went in, and a lot of us got cast. And then we came out here together (WPGH). One of us was prosperous enough to have a car, I forget which one, it might have been David Early, he always had an actual job, and we came out in a car pool.

I remember going to the wrong place at first, Channel 11, and then finding this one. I watched the movie for the first time in twenty years last year, and it was like a class reunion, you know I saw all these people I used to know twenty five years ago, really, and wondered what had happened to them since.

The argument between you and David Early was pretty much scripted, right?

It was, yeah. It was very much scripted. We did it pretty quick. You know, one take, and then they'd move the cameras and do another take. Because we rehearsed it pretty well.

David and I had been in some plays together, and I think at that time we were doing THE TRIAL OF THE CANTONSVILLE NINE, or had just finished that, and I played Daniel Berrigan, and I forget what David played, but anyhow we were used to working together, rehearsing together, so he came up to my apartment, once we got our scripts, and we worked it. We rehearsed it, and found where we needed to put the energy, found how it was structured, and how we needed to run up to a peak, then come back down and start all over again, and all that stuff. So we had it pretty well in hand when we came here. We knew our lines, and it was pretty easy to shoot.

George was very nice. He didn't give a lot of direction. I was expecting, like, micro management, you know "Say this word this way", and "I want you to turn when you say that word", but no, he let it flow. He let us do our thing, and he liked what we did, I guess, well enough to keep it.

Can you remember any amusing anecdotes from the shooting?

Wow. That's a tough question. I do remember I got paid Fifty bucks for the day, and I don't think I even got lunch, I don't remember eating here, because we didn't take very long to do, it you know, it was just a couple hours. And it was definitely non-Union, so I've never gotten any residuals. So Fifty dollars, (laughs) and that convention cost me $300, so I'm $250 in the hole. (Laughs)

At the time of shooting, did you have any idea how much impact the film would have on audiences?

I had absolutely no idea. I didn't give the film at the time the respect it deserves. I was an English major in college, and I was doing serious theater, Shakespeare and stuff, and a zombie movie, it was beneath me, you know. (Laughs) Actually it wasn't at all. It's a fine piece of social criticism, and really wonderful entertainment. George knows how to make you jump in your seat, and it's fun to do that, so I have a lot of respect for it now. But I've been amazed by the fans, you know I went online (to HPOTD) to see if anyone knew anything about conventions, and I got emails from England, Sweden, Japan, people just wanting to say hello, or send me a picture, or whatever. Not only the breath of the audience for the film, but the intensity of their devotion to it. This young man that I met just in June, Alex, knows absolutely every detail about the movie. He has an amazing memory and every frame is in his head. His dad told him he was working with me and asked if he knew who I was and Alex said, "Of course I know who David Crawford is. Wow!" So I'm famous, a little bit, in parts of the world.

Have you seen any of the cast or crew members lately?

Yeah. A lot of us are still based in Pittsburgh. I see David Early occasionally, we worked together. There's a big Shakespeare contest at the public theater for the high school and middle school kids every winter, and they'd send out some of the local actors to coach them, and judge the competition, and we worked together in that.

Vince Vok, who was in the TV scene, he was an extra, is still a friend of mine, we stay in touch, he's in New York now. I don't remember if Bill was in this or not, Bill Hinzman, I don't think he was, I think he was just in Night. Well I worked with Bill a lot over the years, he's mostly retired now, but he used to have a studio downtown, and I did a lot of work for him, voice overs and stuff, and on camera narrations, especially back in the 80's and early 90's, when he was very active in that.

I see Joe Shelby, he's a bartender at Heinz Hall, and when I'm doing a show at the Public Theater, sometimes I see him at the 7-11 picking up cigarettes or something. He's a nice guy, Joe. Tom Savini was very nice. One time, my nephew was a very big fan of Savini's, and Tom let us come over to his house in Bloomfield and gave us a tour of the house. And there were all the horror heads, Fluffy and all of them, all over his house. He had this little kid, in a crib, and I thought my God this kid's going to grow up nuts, surrounded by all this gore, but I guess the kid turned out well.

And George, I live about two blocks from George, and I see him once in a while, like at the Giant Eagle and Chris on the street.

What was your involvement with the new DAWN OF THE DEAD DVD?

I did an interview for that. They came into town, from Los Angeles, and interviewed several of us. I know David Early, and Lenny Lies, and Clayton Hill and Sharon Hill, and I'm sure some others as well, those are the ones I saw at the studio, and they did interviews with us. I think they're planning to cut back and forth between David and me today, and David and me in the movie, which should be interesting.

What was your initial reaction when you first saw the film?

I remember going to the premiere, I forget where it was, I'm thinking it was Regent Square, but it could have been downtown, and I remember this is wild. This is intense horror, and it's great fun, but you know, it'll play in a couple of theaters, then die. (laughs) How wrong I was 25 years later. It's just amazing.

Do you think Dr. Foster would have survived?

I think Dr. Foster knew enough about how the zombies operated, that he would be able to escape. I think he'd probably hole up in a cave somewhere and survive off of nuts and berries.

Have you thought about contacting George for a small part in the new *Dead* movie?

I've been meaning to get in touch with George for months now, for one thing to thank him. You know I never did thank him for making me famous, and also to ask him, I run into kids who desperately want to meet him, to find out how they can do that, whether he has an email address that kids can write to, you know, the fans, or whether they just have to wait till he comes to a convention near them.

So, I wanted to make those two points, and also tell him I'm sorry he's not making the film here. But I don't like to press. I don't like to say "Use me, use me, use me". That would be really nice (to be in the new film). I think it would probably add to the fan base, they would enjoy that, the people who know the old movies.

I'll write to him, but I don't think I'll press him to be in his new one.

TASO STAVRAKIS

ACTOR, STUNTMAN

PERSONAL REFLECTIONS

DAWN OF THE DEAD (1978)

© Laurel Entertainment, Inc.

During DAWN we were stationed in a large room for which the only connection to the mall was down a long, narrow corridor. One long night I was left to finish up the zombies in the community room, after that being bored and having heard nothing for some time, I set off down the corridor to find the set. I got about half way when Tom and Gary Zeller came hurtling around the corner from the mall. They were driving a golf cart at high speed, red-eyed and giggling like drunken school girls. The corridor was narrow and my first thought was, "I might just squeeze tight against the wall...", but no, I'd been targeted. "There's Taso! Let's get 'im!"

Shit, here they came, ricocheting back and forth off the walls, cackling like devils. I turned and ran like a rabbit, no good, they were gaining, there were no other doors and the community room was too far. Just before they ran me over and squished me like a toad, I turned to face them, maybe they'll screech to a halt. I even had some smart-assed comment, whatever it was died in birth as they smashed into me, whooping their mad war cries.

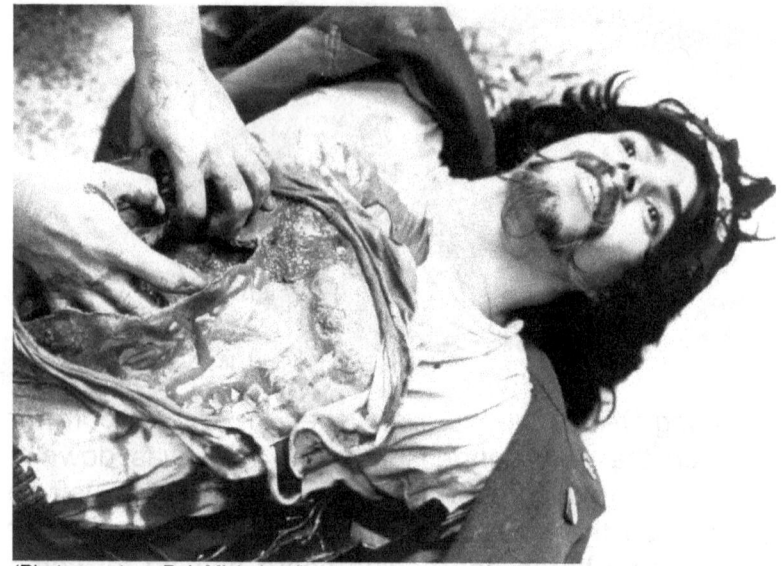

(Photo courtesy Bob Michelucci)   © Laurel Entertainment, Inc.

My instincts saved me; at the last second, I got a foot up onto the front of the golf cart and jumped. The impact knocked me straight up, somersaulting over the cart and those two douche bags, one of my best stunts of the movie and nobody ever saw it.

For years after there were arched black boot prints inexplicably high on the wall and ceiling of that hallway.

MIKE CHRISTOPHER

ACTOR

INTERVIEW BY SERGI

© 2010 by AVANTGUARDA web/zine

DAWN OF THE DEAD (1978)
"HARE KRISHNA ZOMBIE"

© Laurel Entertainment, Inc.

I understand that you studied piano and played with groups. Where did this interest from and when did you learn to play the keyboards?

When I was in 4th grade, I went with my parents to buy a piano. We went to Gimbals Department Store in the north hills, just outside Pittsburgh. They were just starting to sell electric organs at that time. We watched a demonstration and decided to buy an organ instead of the piano. The organ went in the corner of our dining room. I took lessons from a woman named Mrs. Mary Sundholm in the neighboring town of Avalon. I had been taking lessons for about 3 years when I had asked Mrs. Bell, the organist at my church, if I could play some of the services. She, declined my offer and I felt terrible. Strangely enough, a few months later, Mrs. Bell called and asked *me* if I was still interested in playing the organ for the church. Her husband was transferring to another state and the whole family had to move. I said yes and I got the job. It was a bitter sweet moment though, since I had a crush on her daughter Nancy! I became the new organist at Sacred Heart Church in Emsworth and played numerous services there until about two years out of High School. My mother and I would sing a lovely funeral service together. I played there seven days a week... Weddings, funerals, devotions to the Blessed Virgin Mary every Tuesday night, Station of the Cross all thru Lent . . . . it became a home away from home.

Around 1970 I began studying Pipe Organ at the University of Pittsburgh with Dr. Beikman. I later enrolled at the University and studied with Dr. Lord. I left Pitt after completing only one semester when I learned I would not be allowed to take piano and organ lessons at the same time or use the synthesizer studio until Graduate School! The electronic music department had one of the best rooms in the country at that time. They had a four-channel sound system, a Buchla synthesizer, and several reel to reel tape decks. So I quit college and bought an Arp 2600 Synth from a guy who lost his arm in a boating accident and joined a bald band called UFO. UFO was the first incarnation of the space band concept which inspired the FLUID band. As a member of FLUID I had my head shaved which led to being chosen for the Hare Krishna Zombie role.

How were you introduced into the world of the cinema?

Around 1977 or so, the FLUID band began living and rehearsing in the basement of The Leona Theater, an

John Stahl's Million Dollar Theatre opened in Homestead on November 11, 1925. Stahl's was known for its state-of-the-art movie projection and sound system. Marathon dances were held in the basement in the dance land during the 1930s and 1940s. Tituts Hodder took over the building in the 1940s, when hard times hit, and renamed it the Leona Theatre for his daughter. The structure was demolished in 1984 and is home of a national convenience store today.

1,800 seat theater located in Homestead, Pennsylvania just outside of Pittsburgh. Originally named "Stahl's Million Dollar Theater, it cost $1,000,000 when it was first built. The basement had a stage and was used to hold dances when it was first built. The theater was quite run down by 1977 and was showing movies for $1. (I snuck upstairs and saw "Jaws" 14 times in one week!) Joe Shelby (Martinez) from DAWN OF THE DEAD was managing the theater *and* the FLUID band. The New Leona Theater had several store fronts along the street. One of them was a fish store called "Tanks-a-Lot." The large rotund Zombie in DAWN was the owner of the fish store. He also bought a hearse from the FLUID band when we broke up. Lee Cummings was his name, I believe. I guess it was through contacts made at the Leona Theater, FLUID met film makers Mickey Lies, and his brother Leonard Lies who the Machete Zombie in DAWN is. The FLUID band recorded the sound track for A RIDE THROUGH THE FIELDS and HEADPRINTS which were both films made by the Lies brothers. The FLUID band members had lead parts in "Headprints" as well. The connection to Joe Shelby came through John Paul Musser who was the sax player for FLUID as well as the 'Plaid Shirt Zombie' who gets killed while the helicopter lands for fuel. He gets shot right after Ken Foree shoots the kids. 'John Paul' is also the actor whose face is on the DAWN OF THE DEAD poster. Currently, this famous zombie is out of range and cannot be contacted. Clayton Hill, the Escalator/Sweater Zombie ran the security for Fluid band concerts. Unfortunately, Clayton has recently passed away.

Had you already liked films of terror/horror/zombies before acting in DAWN OF THE DEAD?

To be honest I really don't watch many horror films but of course, I knew of George Romero since he was from Pittsburgh. Everyone in Pittsburgh loves NIGHT OF THE LIVING DEAD™. I do remember watching "THE BIRDS" and some other Hitchcock movies as a kid, but mostly I was playing music and didn't watch many movies. My parents didn't let us watch much TV at home. From about 15 years old on, I played in bands and traveled Pennsylvania, Ohio, West Virginia, Maryland and western New York State. I kept very busy with music and just never got interested movies.

Did you study interpretation and drama?

No, I got the part in DAWN because my head was already shaved as part of the theatrical presentation we were doing in 184the FLUID band. Each musician in FLUID was a different color and we beamed on to the stage in a Plexiglas tube which had strobe lights and a little smoke. Originally, I was asked to do the Helicopter Zombie part. At the last minute, I got a call from the DOTD production people who informed me that they had a different part in mind for me. I was a bit disappointed because I wanted to see how the EFX were going to be done but I am glad I got the Hare Krishna Zombie part. It is quite a bit more personal and I got a plastic action figure of my character!

How did they choose you for acting in the film DAWN OF THE DEAD? - How did you get cast for the role of the HARE KRISHNA zombie?

George Romero wanted some different zombies since most of the extras showed up in old shirts and blue jeans. He must have been inspired by my bald head and came up with the idea to make me into a Hare Krishna. My scene was important since I was attacking Fran, one of the main characters. I guess he wanted something special for that. The Krishna's had a temple in Pittsburgh and would clog up the street corners begging money at lunch time. You would find them at the airports as well so; they were an integral part of life in Pittsburgh and other major cities as well. Denver and Los Angeles had temples too.

Before starting to roll film, did GEORGE ROMERO give you any direction on the correct interpretation of your HARE KRISHNA zombie?

Early on, George decided not to tell the zombies how to act. He realized that if he showed people how to drag their foot or tilt their head everyone would drag their foot and tilt their head the same way so he gave the actors the freedom to create their own unique look.

Do you know why GEORGE ROMERO introduced this character into the film? Was it because there were so many HARE KRISHNA in the US at the time?

Well, the Hare Krishna devotees were very annoying. They would start off asking for a dollar for some incense and give you their holy book "for Free" Their book was very heavy. Once you had it in your hands, they would ask for a much larger donation and would refuse to take the book back since they really wanted the money! If you traveled by plane or had to pass them in town all the time the resentment would build up and became extremely frustrating. I'm sure George thought it would be a unique social commentary on popular culture of the day as well as give people a chance to cheer to see one of these guys get their head beat in! Lucky me huh?

Did you know of GEORGE ROMERO and his films? Do you like his type of cinema?

I did not know George prior to DAWN but I saw NIGHT OF THE LIVING DEAD™ so I knew who he was. I like all of George's films especially DIARY OF THE DEAD which reminds me of DAWN I thought " The story was very interesting on its own and the zombies were not the main issue. I'm very selective when it comes to the horror genre. I like THE LOST BOYS, THE DEVILS REJECTS, and 30 DAYS OF

George and Mike at a recent convention

NIGHT for example. "FIDO, SHAUN OF THE DEAD, and ZOMBIELAND I like as well. I'm more attracted to movies like BLADERUNNER, the original ROLLERBALL any of the DUNE movies and THE MATRIX. I like movies that take me to some place I could never get to in reality. I find reading about the politicians, bankers and military contractors who create the conditions for social violence and war much more interesting the fictionalized possibility of horror situations. On the other hand, movies about actual mass murderers make me too uncomfortable since they portray actual events. My girlfriend Shade is heavily into horror and I watch horror movies with it

Would you explain what a typical day of filming for DAWN OF THE DEAD was like? Did you have many hours in make-up?

My make-up was very simple. My head, feet and hands were covered in grey. My make-up didn't really take that long... maybe 10 minutes. I think Tom Savini put on my braided hair piece, but there were so many zombies that needed make-up at the same time it was overwhelming. All of us gathered in this large community room area and there were many people applying grey makeup to the hordes of extras.

I understand that much of the filming took place when it was very cold outside. How was it to work in those conditions?

My scenes were all shot indoors, but I was barefoot, so my feet were freezing. I offered to donate an old pair of sandals to my costume, but they said no. DAWN OF THE DEAD started shooting before Christmas. When the holiday decorations went up, George had to stop shooting for over two months. I had two days of filming in the mall then one day on a set in George's office building. All the scenes at the "hideout" were shot on this set which was constructed in George's office building on Fort Pitt Boulevard. Most of the elevator scenes and my scene with Gaylen and the flare were shot on the set in the office building. The ductwork was also a set which was constructed in George's office building. The mall skylight was actually on top of George's office building and they had to make a replica of it and place it on the roof of the Monroeville Mall.

Did you know in TOM SAVINI? How did he work? Since there were no computer-generated effects back then, was the actual make up frightening?

Yeah, live stunts are dangerous. Tom Savini did quite a few stunts in DAWN. I believe that in most of the stunts where a car or a truck hits a zombie it is Tom Savini who goes flying in the air. I didn't work with Tom on the set at all. I didn't even know who he was until the premier. Tom did his own stunt flying over the railing at the mall. I think he had to do it several times. I like Tom a lot. He's a very interesting fellow. I got to eat dinner with him in London last year in an authentic small pub. I believe the pub was owned by the Young's brewing company and it was originally their house. They opened up the front living room and for a while it was the smallest pub in London or so I heard. Tom and I had a leisurely dinner there just before a convention and that was the only time I've been able to speak with him at length. He's had a remarkable life and has made such a significant contribution to the genre with his acting, EFX and personality. He cracks a mean horse whip too!

What type of relationship did you have with the main characters of the film...Ken Foree, David Emge, Scot Reiniger and Gaylen Ross?

I was a lead zombie which was a step up from being an extra at the time. I didn't socialize with any of the lead actors at the shoot. I pretty much kept to myself. My popularity is directly due to the continued support of the fans. Since I started doing conventions, I have remained in contact with Lenny Lies (Machete Zombie), Joe Shelby (Martinez), Frank Serro (Grey Suit Zombie) who recently passed away, and Jim Krut (Helicopter Zombie). Joe Shelby is in post-production on his film THE GREEN MAN As for the main characters and George Romero, I only see them at conventions. Lenny Lies is operating Dreamcatchers films in Pittsburgh and Michael is working on his new movie BLOOD SPEAR.

Did you know DARIO ARGENTO?

Dario wasn't on the set when I shot my scenes. I never got to meet him.

After finishing filming DAWN OF THE DEAD, did you work in other films?

I lived in Pittsburgh for a while after finishing DAWN OF THE DEAD. The FLUID band broke up and I started electronics school. I was also performing laser light shows for Laserium at the Buhl Planetarium while going to electronics school. Around 1980, I moved to Los Angeles to travel for Laserium then, in 1983, worked for Oberheim Electronics making synthesizers, sequencers and drum machines. I thought about trying to get into films when I lived in Los Angeles but I couldn't get a union card since I did not have a speaking part in DAWN. The extreme popularity of DAWN came many years later. It is the dedication of the fans that made it a cult favorite.

What are your thoughts concerning all of the *Dead* fans around the world?

As far as I'm concerned, the fans of DAWN OF THE DEAD are the best fans in the world. They are mainly responsible for keeping the entire genre of Zombie movies alive (or should I say dead) and should be commended for that. I still find it amazing that the fans are so loyal after all these years. There are three generations of DAWN OF THE DEAD fans coming to the conventions. I know parents who let their kids watch "DAWN" when they were only four years old! Parents sometimes let me hold their baby's and take pictures with them! It is still a mystery to me as to why DAWN OF THE DEAD is still so popular. I guess it is the sheer genius of George Romero. He had the right movie at the right time. I am shocked that I am still able to travel the US. and Europe because of this movie. There is nothing better than being able to talk directly with the fans. Sometimes I have conversations at three in the morning in a hotel lobby or in the hall on my way back to my room. There is the action figure of my character that I still find impossible to believe.

Can you explain some of the more curious things to happen during the filming of DAWN OF THE DEAD?

The most surprising thing that happened to me occurred when Gaylen pointed the flare at me. The flare was very close at times and I had no rehearsal. The hot sulfur sparks were coming at my face and were landing on the floor

Cemetery Zombie meets Hare Krishna Zombie

directly in front of me. I had to walk on them and they were still very hot and glowing! I had to concentrate while my feet were getting burned. I told Gaylen about that at a *HorrorFind 9* convention a few years ago and she said she had no idea that was happening. Another story I've talked about on a few interviews is what I did to get ready for my first scene. I was in character and I walked up a mall security guard and asked him to buy some incense. He said he didn't have his wallet with him and I said "Come on man, it's only a dollar. He said "Really, I keep my wallet in my locker so I won't lose it if I have to run after someone." I pretended to get mad and said, "Look man . . . you have a job, I know you have a god damned dollar!" The security guard had no idea I was just acting. He really thought I was a Hare Krishna! I yelled at him saying" You people are all alike" and walked away. He started following me down the hall of the Monroeville Mall saying "Really man, I want your incense . . . I just don't have any money on me." I knew at that point I was believable as a Hare Krishna.

TOM SAVINI

ACTOR,
SPECIAL MAKE-UP EFFECTS GENIUS,
DIRECTOR

INTERVIEW BY TERROR TRANSMISSION

DAWN OF THE DEAD (1978)
DAY OF THE DEAD (1985)
NIGHT OF THE LIVING DEAD (1990)

© Laurel Entertainment, Inc.

How did you first become interested in horror?

My cousin turned me onto Famous Monsters magazine and then I saw what the real Lon Chaney looked like as the Phantom and as the hunchback, but it was the movie man of 1000 faces that inspired me to want to create monsters because I saw James Cagney as Lon Chaney creating monsters.

What did you parents think about you creating monsters in the house?

Well, my dad was like Tom get that shit off your face, but my mother was totally behind it. She used to let me sneak down on Wednesday nights after my dad went to bed at around nine o'clock and watch a program called SHOCK THEATER with a host named Sir Roger. So my mother was totally behind me doing the makeup. She would even give me money for supplies. I would also have shined shoes to make some money to buy makeup supplies. I would have to take two streetcars and a bus to get to the store downtown to buy the makeup. I used mainly household items like nail polish and toilet paper. But once I discovered spirit gum then it was a whole new ballgame because I could begin gluing on bald caps and stuff like that.

Your next discovery I guess would be that of Dick Smith.

Yeah but that was after I did DAWN OF THE DEAD. I know I didn't know him then, because the blood that I used was the 3m blood. It looked like melted crayons and it was horrible!

The makeup I used was all gray but sometimes the different lighting would make it look blue or green it hardly ever looked gray because of some of the filters that the gaffer was using. It was a big mistake. They were gray and they were supposed to look gray.

(Photo by Bob Michelucci)

Remember it was a sequel to NIGHT OF THE LIVING DEAD™ and my only intention was to make them stand out from those who were living and that means they were supposed to be gray. The idealists to just make all these people look gray and you were supposed to be afraid of them because they were gray. I actually did my best zombies in day of the dead. They were different colors and disintegrating differently. I did a lot of research as how people die and decompose differently depending upon your ethnic group or whether you died in the attic or in the basement. But then they called me on the carpet because the zombies didn't all look the same... But they shouldn't look all the same. They died differently. I won the Academy of science fiction fantasy and horror films Saturn award for day of the dead because of the zombies

Do you still keep in touch with George Romero?

I think we did nine films together. I see them at conventions all of the time and we chat every now and then.

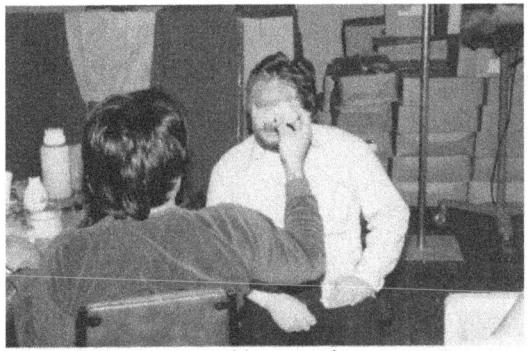

Tom applying my zombie wound. (Photo by Dee Michelucci)

RALPH LANGER

ACTOR

PERSONAL REFLECTIONS

DAWN OF THE DEAD (1978)
DAY OF THE DEAD (1985)
NIGHT OF THE LIVING DEAD (1990)

MY "DAWN OF THE DEAD" EXPERIENCES

In 1977, I was teaching Art and Film-Making classes at North Hills High School, a suburb of Pittsburgh, Pa. I had read they were filming a sequel to NIGHT OF THE LIVING DEAD™, but I really didn't pay much attention to it.

I was attracted to the world of the movies because of my father, a Pittsburgh steel worker. He had been taking regular 8mm home movies starting in 1940. My whole life was documented in his home movies. He allowed me to use his movie camera when I was in 8th grade to film the aftermath of a tornado that hit my neighborhood. Soon after, I was experimenting trying to duplicate what I saw in the movies with my Dad's movie camera. He also taught me a sense of Film History when famous actors, some from the silent era, came on TV in the 1950's.

I was trained to be an Art Teacher. When one of my students heard I had experience with 8mm movie cameras, he asked if I would sponsor a Film-Making Club after school. I agreed, and it became successful. A year later, my school was looking for new classes to expand their Art Curriculum. They asked if I would consider writing a proposal for a Film- Making Class. I wrote the proposal, and it was accepted. Today, almost every school has a digital film making class, but in 1974, it was rare to have a class like this in a high school. The school bought me 5 super 8 cameras, 5 tripods, a dolly, a sound projector, and 100 cartridges of super 8 movie film, with film processing, and I started a 30 year career teaching film making to high school students. Super 8 eventually died out and turned to video.

Video turned to digital computer editing. It was a constantly metamorphosing medium. My students got quite good at making movies and videos. They started entering their films into, and winning Film Festivals, including The Fangoria Film Festivals thru their "Cinemagic" Magazine. My students and I even wrote articles about our films that were published in "Cinemagic" Magazine.

One day at school, the English Teacher, Sue Purviance came over to me, and she was excited. She told me they were looking for zombie extras to show up at closing at the Monroeville Mall for all night filming while the Mall was closed.

When I got home, I told my brother about it. He was excited about it. Since it was a Friday, I went to a relaxing party. I told my friends about zombies being needed at the mall. I was kind of surprised that some of them wanted to go. I really did not feel like going. I had been up since 6:00 a.m. because of my teaching job, and I did not feel like staying up all. My friends told me it would be an adventure and I was talked into going.

When we got to the Mall, I immediately saw Cliff Forrest, a ex-student of mine. He made the most creative welded metal sculptures. Cliff seemed happy to see me, and he took me over to introduce me to his sister, Christine Forrest (George Romero's future wife). She was the assistant director, and she introduced me to George Romero. I brought my super 8 movie camera with me. George gave me permission to shoot Super 8 home movie footage, and he also invited me back as a "special zombie" to be "shot" with squibs. (Tom Savini basically used condoms filled with fake 3M blood, attached to a gun powder charge that he would place on the zombies to be shot).

It was like Halloween. Everyone was being mass painted up with green make up. Everyone was excited to be in a movie. But at the same time, it was not that big of a deal because it was "local". I mean to us, Monroeville Mall was the shopping mall, NIGHT OF THE LIVING DEAD™ was a local handmade horror film that did good. So it was really not a big deal to most of us living in Pittsburgh. But it was entertaining, and we all had fun and we did our best. The zombies were in a holding cell until needed. But since I was allowed to film the behind the scenes, I would go upstairs, and find hiding places, to film the action from. On the day I was being "shot", my brother filmed me. But he did not film the actual scene where the blood shoots out of me even though it was filmed

MOS, or without sound. So I was kind of disappointed about that.

(Photo courtesy Ralph Langer)

I still have the green shirt with the fake blood stains as a souvenir. It is behind me on a shelf with other props from other movies I have worked on. And, it was MY shirt that got ruined that day. They did not have costumes for the zombie extras. We wore whatever we had on. They "scored" 2 asterisk "*" looking cuts in the front of my shirt where the blood would squirt out. They duct taped 2 Squibs that are condoms filled with fake 3M blood, onto a metal plate that was used to protect my skin from being burned when the charge exploded. The gun powder charges were connected to the condoms. They threaded the detonation wires under my shirt, around my back, down through my pants, and out of the bottom of my pants leg. They rubber cemented the "score holes" of the shirt closed. I put the shirt on, and the blood filled condoms were right beneath each of the closed cut score cuts on the shirt. They connected the wires coming out of my leg to a electric "Nail Board". When they tapped a wire to the nail, it set off an electric charge EXPLODING the gun powder breaking the blood-filled condom. The liquid had nowhere else to go, so it squirted through the pre-cut holes in my shirt. I had one problem. I did not have my glasses on while filming. I could not see a thing. I heard George Romero say "ACTION", and I did my zombie shuffle. I heard a LOUD blank gunshot go off, so I reacted to it, and started to flinch and react. The problem was, they did not hit the nail board at the same time as the blank gun shot. So the blood started to squirt out AFTER I reacted to being shot. So my not so "great acting" caused my big scene to be cut from the movie. I do have a close up in the film. But, this one ended up on the cutting room floor unfortunately. But, I kept my ruined shirt as a souvenir. The strange thing is, when I took that ruined shirt home, it was really garbage. But today, there is such a active interest in this cult movie, I bet that I could sell it on Ebay.

My brother Bob Langer, Bill Smith, his then girlfriend, Rita, his sister Janie Krayvo, and her husband Walt Krayvo came to Monroeville Mall with me for our group zombie experience.

My next scene was filmed on the Monroeville Mall Ice Skating Rink. It is now gone. It is a Food Court now. Back then, there were Christmas decorations all around it, but they either moved them, or shot the scene so they could not be seen. I walked on the ice with the other zombies. A few zombies fell. I don't think this was on purpose because the ice was very slippery. Then I was ready for my close up. I play a stupid zombie stuck in a hockey net at the end of the ice. This was my close up in the movie.

My friend, Bill Smith was shot through the head for his scene. Mortician's Wax (or nose putty) was sculpted on his temple. A button size hole was dug out of the wax. The inside of this "hole" was painted black. A button tied to a piece of fishing line was inserted into this hole. Then the Mortician's Wax plug was placed back in and blended smooth and green make up was

(Photo courtesy Ralph Langer)

applied. It looked like he had fishing line coming out of the side of his forehead. They placed a condom filled with the fake 3M blood on the back of his head with a metal plate protecting his skull from where the explosion would be. A small detonation wire was connected to the "Squib", or Gun Powder Charge, to the condom filled with blood. This cord went down the back of Bill's shirt and pants, and over to a nail board. When it was electrified, a metal contact wire hit the nail connected to this wire, and the electricity caused the gun powder to explode, breaking the condom squirting the fake blood out of the back of his head, and onto a plate glass window behind him. When they filmed, they pulled the button out by pulling the fishing line, making it look like he was shot in the head. It looked like the bullet exploded through his head. Bill was literally dripping with fake blood, as it dripped down the back of his shirt. It was in his hair, and all over him. (Again, this was done safely with thick metal protecting his head from the explosion. So don't go putting explosives next to your head. If anyone did that, this would not be a "Special Effect").

After zombie Bill Smith was shot in the head, the fake blood splashed all over the store window and floor behind him. There was a ever present clean-up crew with mops, buckets, water, and rags to clean the windows, floors, and anything else that was splattered with fake blood.

Walt Kravo bit a big chunk out of someone's neck in the film. I later found out that it was biker, Marty Schiff, that Walt bit. They created a foam rubber wound in Marty's neck. They put aquarium hosing from the wound opening, hidden down his shirt, and out of the bottom of his shirt. It connected to a large syringe filled with fake blood. When the syringe was pumped, the fake blood would squirt out of his fake neck wound. The problem was, when George Romero yelled "Action", Walt bit the foam rubber off of the wound, but he also bit into the aquarium hose and he started to pull it out of the wound like a long vein. I did not know this at the time, but Marty Schiff recently said on Facebook, "This was the second and last take. On the first take Walt missed the perforation for the bite and was actually biting my real shoulder through the appliance. I yelled "cut" because of the pain. George was confused because he was into the realism of my "acting". In the edit the screams are from the first take".

So my brother Bob, Bill, Walt, and I made it into the movie; Janie and Rita did not.

My brother Bob is in the scene where zombies are sitting on the ground, next to the second-floor mall railing, eating large ham bones with bits of ham on them as a girl zombie walks past holding a leg.

Assistant make-up artist and zombie, Jeanie Jefferies took a Polaroid photo of my brother Bob and I as zombies. Bob knew Andy Warhol's nephew, Jamie Warhola. Jamie was a up and coming artist like his uncle. When QUESTAR Magazine publisher, Bob Michelucci created his movie tie in magazine of the "DAWN OF THE DEAD POSTERBOOK" movie poster magazine, Jamie Warhola created one of the posters. He used the photo of me from the Polaroid, and a photo of my brother sitting eating the hambone. So my brother and I both were in this poster book.

At the end of the night, I remember it was snowing outside, and at dawn when I went to my car, my tire was flat. So Bill Smith and I had to change the tire before going home after staying up all night. But what I remember from DAWN OF THE DEAD, was it was like a party atmosphere for the crew, and for the zombies. It was fun. And the crew and Director, George Romero, all seemed to be having a great and relaxed fun time. It was SO EASY to be a Zombie. All

(Photo courtesy Ralph Langer)

you had do was show up at Monroeville Mall when it closed at night, they took your name, and gave you a dollar for pay. I was very lucky to be at the right place at the right time. And now I am part of a very famous cult movie.

A few weeks later, George Romero called my home. He said they were having a cast and crew screening of the last movie they did, "Martin" and he wanted to know if I wanted to attend. I was kind of in shock that George Romero was calling me at home, but I managed to say "Yes" in a very calm way. Most of the crew from DAWN OF THE DEAD was there too.

Another thing happened a few weeks after filming Pittsburgh Channel 53, played NIGHT OF THE LIVING DEAD for the first time...uncut.... on network TV. That was something no one expected, because that film was still pretty much out there, back then. No one ever thought it would ever play on TV at that time.

Jeanie Jefferies took the Polaroid photo of me and my brother Bob Langer and Bob was lucky enough to have been painted into the DAWN OF THE DEAD posterbook illustration that was done by James Warhola (Andy Warhol's nephew) (Photo courtesy Ralph Langer)

The local film critic, George Anderson, interviewed George Romero during the commercial breaks. And after the movie, they started to talk about the recently completed DAWN OF THE DEAD and George Romero showed clips, and uncut footage that still had the clapboards attached. This was way before the movie finally came out.

There was so much footage and behind the scenes of the George Romero movies shot in Pittsburgh shown local TV stations and Local Programs throughout the years. This footage is now very rare and hard to come by. I always wondered why they did not use this footage in the "behind the Scenes" of the DVD's of the Romero movies?

I had my super 8 home movies processed and I edited them. They showed things like the teenage boy who gets shot in the forehead with a arrow. It was filmed in reverse but was cut from the film. Pittsburgh Steeler, Franco Harris was visiting the set that night. I filmed George Romero blowing out the candles on the wrap cake. It must have been the last day of filming because the cast and crew also posed for their group photo wearing their black DAWN OF THE DEAD tee shirts. The huge window that was broken because of a overly large explosion was all captured on my super 8 movie camera. I had a problem with the film though. I used Kodak's new super 8 film stock "Ektachrome 160Type G". It was good for low light filming, but, for some reason, as it ages, it grows a irritating looking crystalline pattern all over the film. They said the only way to get rid of it was to reprocess the film. I had that done, and it immediately started to grow back. Unfortunately, it was on this film that I learned the hard lesson to never use this film stock again.

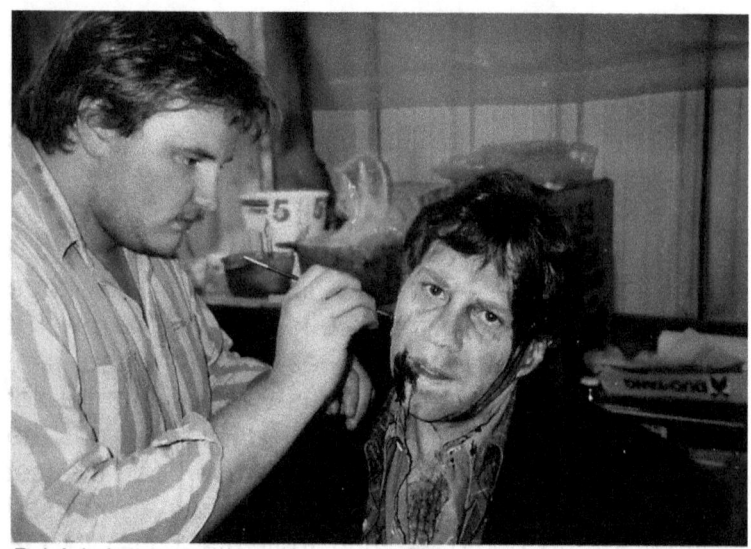

Ralph being made up as a zombie for NIGHT OF THE LIVING DEAD™ 1990   (Photo courtesy Ralph Langer)

I showed this movie to my film making students, but after a while it just sat on my shelf along with a lot of other films and home movies. One day, my brother called from Los Angeles and told me he heard Anchor Bay was going to distribute a 4 disk DAWN OF THE DEAD DVD set, and they wanted to use my home movie. He wanted me to send it to him, so they could have it digitally transferred. I sent the film to him. I was not in LA, so my brother said, he was going to do the commentary for the home movie. Unfortunately, when they released the DVD set, they did not put my

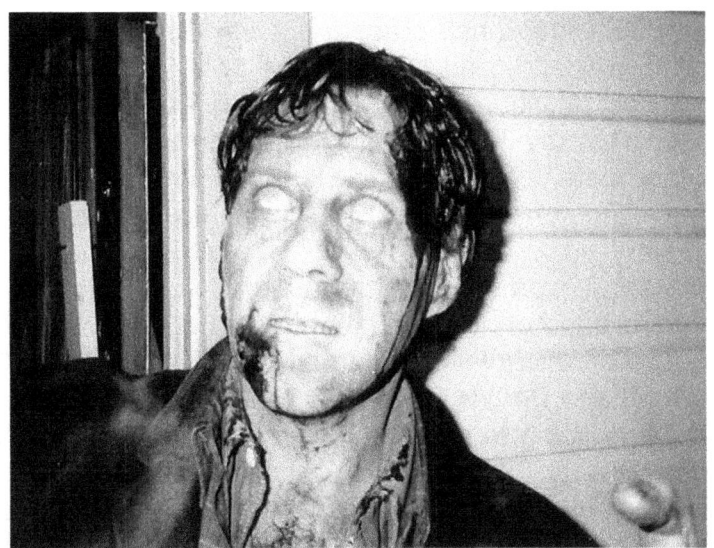

Ralph as a zombie in NIGHT OF THE LIVING DEAD™ (1990)
(Photo courtesy Ralph Langer)

name as a credit on the DVD. Some of the reviews mentioned me, but none of the advertising. What can you do? I guess I should have gone to LA to be part of the commentary. So my home movie is on Disk 4 of the Anchor Bay set, and they used some of my footage in the new DAWN OF THE DEAD documentary, but I am not given credit. (Film maker Rusty Nails is making a documentary on George Romero, and he asked me to let him use the footage. I agreed, so I hope it will be part of his documentary, with credit this time). But, then again, the credit really goes to George Romero, who actually allowed me to film this footage. Plus, it was originally meant to be shown to my students.

When the movie DAWN OF THE DEAD came out, they also released a hardback book novelization of the movie, written by George Romero and Suzanne

Sparrow. When I heard about it, I went to Jay's Book Stall in Oakland, and I bought the only 5 copies the store had. I figured it would be a great Christmas present for my friends who were zombies. I had another idea. I went over to George Romero's Latent Image office on Fort Pitt Blvd. I got into the elevator and went up to his floor. The elevator door opened, and George was standing there alone next to a desk. He got a huge grin on his face, and said, "Hi how are you doin?" which was his normal greeting. I told him I bought these DAWN OF THE DEAD hardback books, and I was going to give them to my friends who went to the DAWN OF THE DEAD filming with me, and they were also zombies. I figure, they would be great Christmas presents. He happily signed and personalized them all. Then he looked at me and asked, "Why don't you want one?" I told him these were the entire store had in stock, and I wanted to give them out as presents. He went into a room and came out with one of the hardback books and he signed one to me. This is one of my greatest possessions, and I will keep it forever. George wrote "Thanks for being a zombie" in all of the books. Again, these books are now rare even without the autographs. It is funny how things raise in value as the years go on. I have been keeping these mementos on a shelf and in my photo albums for years. But it seems today, many people get a kick out of seeing this kind of thing since zombies are in vogue again. . For years, no one really cared about any of this. I guess it is the resurgence of zombie movies and TV shows that reminded everyone of how this all started. And credit should be given where credit is due. And that is with George Romero, who started all of this. And he was nice enough to throw those of us who were adventurous enough to stay up all night at

Monroeville Mall, into a kind of Romero Zombie Hall of Fame.

This creative invention of George Romero is relevant because ALL of the newer zombie movies have copied this mythology that Romero INVENTED. George also put zombies into a shopping mall. Many people forget this, but shopping malls were a fairly new concept back when DAWN OF THE DEAD was filmed. Downtown Pittsburgh was the shopping Mecca back then. If you needed clothes, or if you wanted to shop, or see a movie, you took a bus or drove to Pittsburgh, to buy them at a Department store. But all of a sudden newly invented mall like South Hills Village Mall and Monroeville Mall were built, stealing shoppers from the city to the suburbs; and they had free parking. The ironic thing is, people travel from all over the USA, and from other countries just to visit the Monroeville Mall just because DAWN OF THE DEAD was filmed there. But the majority of people who live here in Pittsburgh really DO NOT CARE. The people who live here just go to Monroeville Mall to shop, not even thinking or caring that there was a famous cult zombie movie filmed there. The people who run the mall look at zombie fans as a inconvenience. If you start using a video camera in Monroeville Mall, the mall security will immediately descend upon you, and will firmly tell you that you are NOT allowed to video tape in the mall. So this local zombie phenomenon seems to be more popular in other cities, and other countries, than it is here with most of Pittsburgh. I guess people here grew up with this, and most do not care, or they are just used to it.

This experience also started a professional relationship between George Romero, Christine

Romero, and my film making classes. Chris was a alumni of North Hills High School, the school I taught at. So whenever George made a movie in Pittsburgh, he always invited my film making students to come over to observe. They were treated like royal guests on all of his film sets.

On the DAWN OF THE DEAD set   (Photo courtesy Ralph Langer)

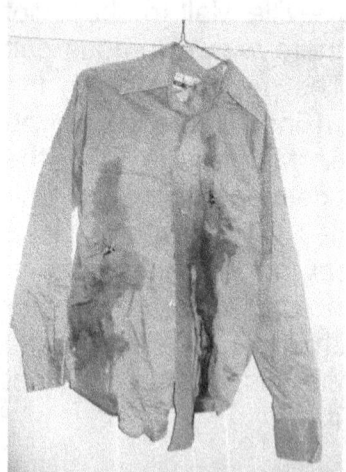

Ralphs blood stained zombie shirt (Photo courtesy Ralph Langer)

MARTY SCHIFF

ACTOR

PERSONAL REFLECTIONS

DAWN OF THE DEAD (1978)

© Laurel Entertainment, Inc.

AS I REMEMBER IT...

When it was my time to die in DAWN...Tom had placed tubing on my shoulder then glued a prosthetic shoulder to my real shoulder over the tube. He perforated the exact spot where the "zombie" was to bite me. On the first take the camera was rolling and the zombie missed the perforation and bit into my actual shoulder...I was screaming in pain and called "CUT!!!" myself. George confused said "Marty...what are you doing?" I said "He's biting my REAL shoulder!!" George laughed and said..."Looked great". The second take...he got the tube in his teeth. And blood was being pumped into my ear. Slow down the DVD at that moment and you can see it.

Taking a break on the set of with Tom Savini (Photo courtesy Marty Schiff)

With Tom Savini again, this time in CREEPSHOW
© Laurel Entertainment, Inc. (Photo courtesy Marty Schiff)

JIM KRUT

ACTOR

INTERVIEW BY MIKE GENCARELLI

Conducted February 14, 2011

DAWN OF THE DEAD (1978)
"HELICOPTER ZOMBIE"

© Laurel Entertainment, Inc.

Jim Krut is well known for his small but very notable role as the Helicopter Zombie in DAWN OF THE DEAD. Since then Jim has not done many films but he has been quite involved with the genre. Movie Mikes had a chance to ask Jim a few questions about his working on DAWN OF THE DEAD and his career.

Tell us how you got the role of the Helicopter Zombie in DAWN OF THE DEAD?

I got the role of Helicopter Zombie in DAWN OF THE DEAD when Tom Savini asked me to do the role. At the time, I was living in the Oakland section of Pittsburgh, working in live theater with a traveling repertory company called the Ironclad Agreement. I was literally on my way to see a movie in Oakland, when I ran into Tom. Tom said, "Jim I have a great role for you in the George Romero film that's being made here in Pittsburgh. I think you'll really like it." I told him, "Tom, in a few minutes I'll be in a movie."

Tom said, give me a call and we'll set up the makeup sessions.

How long have you know Tom Savini?

Tom and I had had known each other for a number of years, since we were in college together in Pittsburgh. There, we acted in student productions. Tom and I were the two actors in a version of Edward Albee's *The Zoo Story*. During that run, the real knife that we used made a real impact on Tom's midsection. But, as they say, show must go on. Tom didn't flinch; we finished the show and no one ever knew that he'd been injured.

Tell us about the makeup process for your character?

We got together for the makeup sessions in Tom's workshop, in the basement of his home. He needed to do a head cast of me. This entailed my breathing through a straw for about 20 minutes while plaster was slathered all over my face until it hardened. Then, the back of the head was done the same way. It helps you appreciate the old movies where fugitives are hiding in a stream and breathing through a hollow reed while they stay concealed. In this case, however, Tom called me a few days later and said that the plaster cracking we need to repeat the process. I returned to Tom's workshop. He completed the plaster molding of my head and from that was able to build the rest of the prosthetics. To make the removable headpiece proportional to the rest of my head, Tom applied the beard, mustache and a bit more hair. It seems like only a few days from that point that we were on set at the Monroeville airport.

How long did it take to shoot your scene?

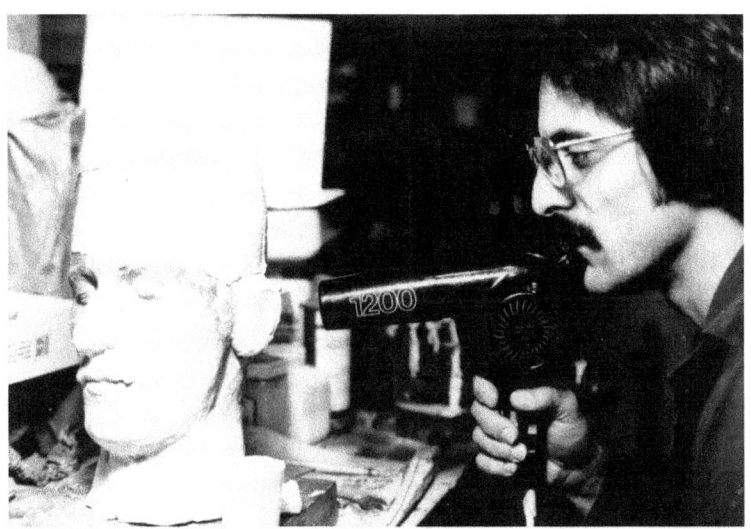
Tom Savini working on the head appliance (Photo courtesy Bob Michelucci)

In my recollection, I was there two days. The first day was pretty drizzly and a lot of the indoor shooting was done at that time. There may have been some uncertainty about the helicopter arriving if there was rain. I believe the first shooting day at the Monroeville airport was a Sunday and I pretty much stayed inside the little office building for most of that. It gave me a chance to watch how others were working and how George Romero was directing. It was my first time on a movie set. As a struggling actor in Pittsburgh, it was also great to have access to the lunch wagon from craft services. As for the costume, there were at least two identical sets of clothes for me. We only needed one, since everything was done in one take. Applying the makeup and appliances took about an hour, as I recall. Tom had everything ready to go and seemed to be everywhere on the set at the airport. As for direction, I believe that Tom had worked far enough in advance with George that George trusted Tom to pull off the effect. I'm pretty sure George directed all of the camera angles, but Tom worked on the timing and the execution of the effect. Again, everything was done in one take. Time may have been a factor, but everything seemed to go very smoothly because of the earlier planning. Both Tom and I are Vietnam veterans. We were both familiar with helicopters from that experience. Stepping up onto the loosely arranged boxes, while focusing on the "meat" refueling the helicopter was probably the trickiest part of the shot for me. I wanted it all to be right. Even if this would be my only time ever in a movie, I was going to give it my best. It was surprising, but very gratifying; to learn we didn't have to repeat the shot. People on the set said it looked great and seemed to be really happy with the way it turned out. I believe the shooting involving the Helicopter Zombie scenes took about an hour altogether.

Although being in the film for only a short time, you character is definitely well-known form the series, how do you feel about that?

As for being so well known for this relatively short sequence in a cult film, all I can say is I'm extremely happy to have been a part of it! You have to remember, at the time; George Romero was breaking a lot of new ground. From what I saw of the effects, language and action, I figured that my family and friends at the time might never go to see this movie but, that's what taking a chance is all about. I'll

© Laurel Entertainment, Inc.

always be grateful to Tom Savini for including me in this movie. My being part of this George Romero classic has since become a huge source of conversation and pride for my family and friends. Once the shooting was done, and then came the nervous before the screening in downtown Pittsburgh. Inside the packed theater were the actors, crew, friends and hundreds of zombies it seemed. There was the nervous anticipation of wondering if my scenes would actually make it up onto the big screen or end up on the cutting room floor. It was a huge thrill to see how the scene worked into the grand scheme of DAWN OF THE DEAD.

You didn't do many films post DAWN, what was the reason?

Within a year after the release of DAWN, I was married to my wife Linda. When our first daughter was born, we left Pittsburgh to find a place with cleaner air and less traffic. We settled in central Pennsylvania, where I worked for a time in audiovisual sales for 3M Company. Then I was hired as an editor for a weekly newspaper, making use of my journalism degree from Point Park University. Within two years we moved to the Harrisburg, Pennsylvania area. There I had a job as editor of the statewide magazine for the Pennsylvania Rural Electric Association. I love the work and travel, but it didn't leave time for other pursuits such as acting on stage or in film. Seven years later we moved to Gettysburg, where I became involved with a startup theater company. Around the year 2000, I was invited to Cinema Wasteland in Cleveland, from DAWN OF THE DEAD reunion. It was great to see some friends I worked with in theater in Pittsburgh, who also happen to have been in DAWN OF THE DEAD. It was also a chance to get to know some of the other actors from the movie. The really amazing thing, however, was the fans. I knew DAWN had become a cult classic, but it was hard to appreciate just how widespread the reach of that movie had become. For the Cleveland show, someone had flown in from Japan. People had driven in from California, Texas, New Jersey and other states. It was overwhelming! I'll always be grateful to Ken Kish, who runs Cinema Wasteland, for tracking me down and bringing me back to the public eye! That horror convention led to other appearances over the last several years. Between those appearances and some of my theatrical performances, I was asked to take on roles in other movies. First came THE GUATEMELAN HANDSHAKE in which I had a small role, but it was great working with the cast and the director. That I met Gary Ugarek, who offered me a lead role in his film DEADLANDS 2: TRAPPED. I love the role and a chance to play an evil government official. It seemed there were so many role models to work from!

Where you a fan of the horror genre before working on the film?

As for being a fan of horror movies, I have been since I was a kid. I would stay up late at night and watch them on television. I would go to the movies and watch DRACULA, FRANKENSTEIN, THE WOLFMAN, and more on the big screen. The Thing, Them, all sorts of monsters and creatures! Boris Karloff, Lon Chaney, and the classic horror actors were my idols. My scene from DAWN OF THE DEAD has been classified by Bravo Network as one of the top 100 moments in horror movies. No matter what else I've done or where I've traveled, nothing seems to be as well known in my life as the role of the Helicopter Zombie. It's absolutely been great! And, I remain grateful to Tom Savini, George Romero and especially the fans who helped to keep the "dead" alive!

What else are currently working on?

I've done a few other independent films since then. One was a short, SQUIRREL that has not yet been released but has appeared at a few film festivals. Another, DEAD ISLAND was directed by Josh Davidson. He shot the entire feature-length film on iPhones. That was just a few months ago. Another indie film, with the working title of BUNNYMAN BRIDGE, was being shot entirely with digital SLR cameras. I'm not sure about the release date on those. There was also Joe Shelby's THE GREEN MAN being shot in Pittsburgh. Joe was one of the motorcycle raiders in DAWN OF THE DEAD. I'll have just a brief appearance.

RANDY KOVITZ

ACTOR

DAWN OF THE DEAD (1978)

© Laurel Entertainment, Inc.

How did you first get involved with Dawn of the Dead?

I auditioned just as I was finishing up my training at the CMU School of Drama. It was down in George's offices on Fort Pitt Blvd.

How did you end up doing make-up and acting for the film?

I had played the role of the young cop who asks the leads for cigarettes at the police dock in November or December, I believe. I was working in a theater company in Pittsburgh, so I was around as they continued shooting after New Year and I heard that Tom Savini, who I knew because he was at CMU at the same time I was there, was looking for people to help on the make-up crew. I started working for them out at the Monroeville Mall. We'd get there mid-evening, make up Zombies for a few hours and then they'd start shooting. It was great to be able to watch the crew work. My work consisted mainly of applying grey pancake make-up to any skin that would be showing on a Zombie (This was a big job with the fat zombie in the swim trunks), then Tom or one of the other, more skilled people would put on the finishing touches. Later in the process, I had grown a beard for a play I was doing. I borrowed a leather jacket and some mirrored sunglasses and showed up one night when I knew they'd be shooting biker stuff. George didn't recognize me at first, but when he did, he said "Hey, Randy, wanna work tonight?" Of course, I did, and I wound up dodging wax bullets that they were shooting at some breakaway glass above my head, breaking some bottles over Zombies heads and generally having a blast.

What parts (or types of parts) did you play?

Lately, I've been playing character roles, like a sadistic film director in a film called BREAKING CHARACTER, a grumpy wheelchair-bound German scientist who judges a school science fair in the Nickelodeon series *Supah Ninjas* and the election commissioner in the 2012 season finale of NBC's *Parks and Recreation*. But for most of the nearly 20 years I was in L.A., I've also played doctors and lawyers on shows like *E.R* and *The Practice*

What were your experiences going between make-up artist and acting?

I never really worked as a make-up artist after DAWN. I did my own make-up for various stage plays, or course and my work as a fight director afforded me the opportunity to coordinate a lot of special effects, but make-up was never something I pursued as a career.

Were there any interesting experiences on the set either as actor or make-up artist?

When we were shooting at the police dock we kept getting ready to roll and then it would start to snow, so we'd have to wait until it stopped for continuity. It was my very first film job and my first time on a set. I was 21 and had no idea that I should take it easy with the coffee and donuts they had for us. It was about 3 in the morning when we started and I had been there for hours already. Between the caffeine, sugar and adrenaline, I was pumped. Adding to all of that, I was psyching myself up before we rolled so I'd have the emotional "juice" for the scene. After about the third time they cut just before we shot, I realized I would burn out if I kept up the intensity. So after that, I waited until we were rolling, asked for a minute to prepare and then started the scene. It was a valuable acting lesson and I have used what I learned ever since -- especially the part about laying off the donuts on set.

How do you now look back at those times?

They were wonderful times -- thrilling and novel to me as a stage-trained actor. It was the last year in Pittsburgh for me before moving to New York and I was working all the time. That year I did eight plays DAWN OF THE DEAD and a TV movie, I was looking at the industry with innocent eyes, not really know what I was a part of. The fact that so many people, world-wide have been affected by the work we did is very gratifying. But back then, we had no idea. We were just happy to be working.

JEANIE
JEFFERIES

ACTOR, MAKE-UP ARTIST

PERSONAL REFLECTIONS

DAWN OF THE DEAD (1978)
"BLONDE ZOMBIE"

© Laurel Entertainment, Inc.

I was in a Holiday Inn one Saturday evening, handing out samples of one of Iron City's new beers, when I went up to a table of several gentlemen. After I did my 'beer thing', one of the gentlemen asked me if I was interested in interviewing for a radio project that was coming up for WTAE Radio. I said yes!! He gave me his business card, (he was the general manager) and we set up a time for me to come in on Monday. It was actually going to be a fun project for their FM station, 96KX. I got the job and became the 96KX Call Girl! Sounds funny, doesn't it! ha ha The next year was filled with my either making phone calls from the station, or appearing on the streets with a mic in my hand, asking strangers "What is your favorite radio station"? If they responded 96KX....I would tell them who I was and give them a $100.00 bill!! I was very popular!! ha ha   I loved that assignment...a whole year of hosting parties and making people richer.

One party was in October. I was going to find the best Halloween Costume, and award that person $100.00.

Well, a lot of good costumes, but I was taken with one in particular. It was a tall Darth Vader. I picked it. When it was time for me to interview this costumed person, Darth needed to take off his costume face. It turned out to be Tom Savini! (Of course, I did not know a thing about who Tom was or what he did). Long story short, we chatted quite a bit, and he invited me to help him do make-up for DAWN OF THE DEAD....I was very happy to agree to that, for I DID know of George Romero, and working with his cast and crew, would be wonderful !

I missed the first two weeks of the filming of DAWN, but caught on right away. I had a lot of experience doing 'straight' make-up, for I was a make-up artist for photography and TV spots, but to my delight, I found I has some natural ability to create special effects as well! Cool!

Tom and I, and others, would create some gruesome effect, and then sit around thinking how to top it! It was soooo much fun for me. George Romero was the nicest, calmest and well, such a gentleman to work with. I was also very impressed with Mike Gornick, the camera man. In fact, I was impressed with all the crew. Everyone was so professional, and we were a team. And one thing with George....if you did a good job, you would be working with him on the next movie project. What a fun life I have had. I am very grateful to have made such nice friends. To this day, Joe Shelby has remained a great buddy of mine. And recently I got to see Nick Tallo, John Amplas and Bob Michelucci again. That was a highlight!! (Love these guys!!) On Face Book, I have chatted with Lennie Lies, and Galen Ross.

My first days of working with DAWN, was the helicopter scene, and the kids at the airport. I had a ball, and couldn't wait to do more and more and more! Doing the different locations was fun for me too. We would be in one place, and then make it look like another location when the actors walked through a door. The folks that were in charge of continuity sure had their hands full!

One cool memory was when I was renting an 90 acre farm, during the filming of DAWN OF THE DEAD. I had a horse, dog, cat, and the land also had a nice lake on it. Well....one morning, I could hear all this racket outside. I looked out my bedroom window, and there was Tom Savini and Taso Stavrakis, playing with swords, and jousting in my dirt driveway. They were having a ball! You have to admit...things like that just don't happen to a common girl.

Bob and I have worked on several projects together...in fact, I was his 'resident' Scream Queen! I'll let Bob share those days with you.....but I sure have some GREAT memories from those projects we worked on together!!! By the way.... he and I have a lot of photos that we can both sign for you, if that sounds like something you would like to own.

Working on DAWN OF THE DEAD was fascinating. We sure left AND cleaned up a lot of blood in the Monroeville Mall! I recently moved and found a bottle of my original 3M Simulated blood, that I used in DAWN. I have made necklace vials with it, so I can share that 'moment in that time with people'. Let me

Jeanie and George Romero   (Photo courtesy Jeanie Jefferies)

know if you would like one.

When it's gone...it's gone. Wasn't DAWN OF THE DEAD a great movie??? It is so much better than some of the new horror flicks. I think that people actually cared about the characters. My job was to work very closely with the actors. My husband laughs when we watch the movie...I'll tell him "I was sitting right on the corner of the bed when Mike filmed that".....or "I was standing RIGHT there when he was being torn apart"!!! Tom and I would go to the butcher stores to get bones....then we'd put bread on them when the scene to be shot. It would look as though the Zombies were pulling off flesh and eating it.

Squibs being placed on Jeanie.   (Photo courtesy Bob Michelucci)

I remember one evening feeling weird that I didn't have grey pancake make-up on, for there were so many Zombies walking around.

I grew up loving *Twilight Zone* and *The Outer Limits* Working on DAWN was just too much fun! We began doing make-up in the evening; right after the Monroeville Mall closed and worked all night. Then we needed to have everything clean and us out

Jeanie poses with author Bob Michelucci in alternate zombie make-up (Photo by Dee Michelucci)

of there about 8am. Some of us would hit the restaurants and order spaghetti.... sounded weird to the waitresses, but it was dinner time for us. I didn't sleep those 3.5 months. Filming all night, and preparing make-ups during the day time. Plus, we needed to watch the rushes. I never missed sleeping, nor did I lose energy. I was just happy. I was thrilled when George asked me to be in the truck scene. Tom created that make-up for me. The fake eyes and being squibbed both under my mask and on my back was a little eerie for me though. Just think if something would have gone wrong..eeek!

My next film was KNIGHTRIDERS. I was Director of Make-up for that one. I had two assistants, Molly and Liz, who were great ladies to have on board helping me. The pool scene that I was in was actually shot at Molly's Mom and Dad's beautiful house. (That is another cool thing about George, the. crew got to be IN the movies too!!) Imagine working with Ed Harris! I didn't think he and I were going to work together very

The final squib effect.
© Laurel Entertainment, Inc.

(Photo courtesy Jeanie Jefferies)

well. The first day, Ed said under no certain terms that he did not want any make-up on!!! Well, I insisted that he change his mind. I knew I could do a natural look and that he'd like it. I just asked him to try and trust me. Well...I did his make-up every single day...but I always had the feeling he didn't enjoy it. I loved working on Patty Tallman! She was so pretty. I gave my assistant Liz Steven King's make-up to do. I wish now that I could have chatted with him...I never did.

MICHAEL GORNICK

CINEMATOGRAPHER

INTERVIEW EXCERPT FROM
QUESTAR MAGAZINE
1979

DAWN OF THE DEAD (1978)

At age 31, Mike Gornick has established himself as a film generalist of the first rank. Cinematographer, sound man. technician, writer, editor and sometime director for numerous commercial and theatrical projects, Mike's canny knack for filmmaking has proven itself time and again most recently in George Romero's DAWN OF THE DEAD. Despite the rigors of his craft, Mike displays idealism, a modesty and an ethereal charm which are all too uncommon. In the following interview, Mike offers a camera's-eve view of cinematography as both an art form and a way of life.

The media have given much of the credit for DAWN's success to George Romero's directing and Tom Savini's special effects. Still, it would seem that cinematography is just as crucial a factor.

It is. And I feel very fortunate in being recognized in any respect. It hasn't been until the advent of cinematographers like Gordon Willis, Laszlo Kovacs and Vilmos Zsigmond that the director of photography has surfaced 'as a contributor in his own right. Strictly speaking, who ever thought about the cameraman? Who ever thought about Karl Freund shooting anything, like The Last Laugh? I'm serious. He's been an unknown.

George has described you as "an excellent cinematographer who can stack with anyone who's working on the coast," and the visuals for DAWN display a wealth of professional talent. As I recall, though, you didn't break into film with the intention of being a cinematographer.

That's true. I began in this business as a sound man, doing whatever I could. I came to this company in 1972-directlyout of the Air Force, where I had done a lot of editorial work on some strange footage that was coming back from Vietnam. I was trying to piece together a film to demonstrate the fact that the Vietnamese could fly planes-which they can't. I came out of that background to the Latent Image and did sound work for two years. Luckily, there was enough freedom here to try everything. I did some editorial work, writing, directing and filming-then finally moved into cinematography.

Actually, I started out to be a TV weather-man. I just happened to be interested in TV and I liked meteorology, so I thought I might combine the two and become a TV weather expert. I went to Penn State on a scholar-ship in meteorology and got tired of that the first year. Consequently, I dropped out of meteorology to concentrate on' broad-casting and film. When I graduated, I had a lot of knowledge and a paper degree, but very little understanding of the actual mechanics of filmmaking.

After that, I enlisted in the Air Force-on the agreement that I would be assigned someplace where I could get some studio training. After I was in, they said, "You fool! They tell everybody that!" Luckily for me, though, the Air Force kept its promise. After Basic Training, I was transferred to a studio in Los Angeles. I was the only military person there, but we produced' a lot of military films and prepared Congressional Reports on the Vietnamization program. That was during the Nixon administration, when we were teaching the Vietnamese how to fend for themselves-we were going to slip out the back door and they were going to maintain the war. We also made films for the Space and Missile Systems Organization, which is actually NASA. NASA is a kind of public relations front for SAMSO, which-technically speaking-nobody knows about. SAMSO takes all the technology from NASA and applies it militarily.

Anyway, .that's where I really learned filmmaking. I worked with old Hollywood filmmakers who are now 65 years old, retired and comfortable. They let me do all the work, which was great for me. I got all the experience and they just sat back. I got to shoot I got to do editorial work, I got to do sound work-everything.

What was your first involvement with the Latent Image?

I had never heard of George Romero until I saw NIGHT OF THE LIVING DEAD™ at a small underground theater in Denver. Everyone there was excited about it. They were quoting the film and talking about Evans City as if they'd lived there all their lives. So I studied the credit crawl and saw George's name every three feet. I was impressed. It was really a pretty tight film, and well produced.

I had that in the back of my mind when I returned to Pittsburgh from LA I figured I would just stop by the Latent Image, meet George Romero and see what he was all about. When I got there, though, George was out in Evans City filming THE CRAZIES. I spoke with the producer, Al Kroft who said he could use a sound man. I was hired on the spot Two days later I was in Evans City. I handled the sound for half of THE CRAZIES, then was called back to the main studio to fill in for the commercial sound man, who had left Finally, after the feature was completed, I met George and signed on full time. From there-we went on to film more commercial I pieces, including a dozen or so sports documentaries for network TV After that came MARTIN-and now, DAWN.

It's been said that the essential function of the cinematographer is to translate the director's vision of a scene into film. Do you find that your filming technique reflects the influence of George Romero?

I think so. I think on a very gutsy level, though. I don't believe George and I ever spent days rapping philosophies of the film; it either works or it doesn't work. I think there is a rapport, an instant magic that happens spontaneously. George and I commonly share a lot of ideas about art, music, cars, women and what-have-you. We just happen to be in tune with each other. We understand each other. But most importantly, I understand that together we can demonstrate on film exactly what he wants.

There may be a university or a film school. Somewhere that can actually teach people to respond instantly to directors. If that's possible, I don't know about it with me, it's been solely a matter of instinct I have reacted to George very well and it works. Of course, I have my own perceptions of how things should be filmed-but for the most part they happen to coincide with George's.

DAWN was very cleanly photographed, and much use was made of quick cuts and multiple angles. I found it difficult to believe at first that one man could have managed all that. Were economic considerations a big factor in the decision to use only one camera?

Most certainly. But I imagine there was also a little selfishness on my part. I like to shoot everything myself, when possible. I've met very few people in whom I have enough faith to be able to say, "I'll sit back and let you shoot this for me. I'll just set the angle and give you the composition." To simply be a Director of Photography and sit back in my telescope chair and relax, to just point out shots and feel the aesthetics that would be nice in a sense. But there is a certain joy...something really exciting, about making the shots yourself and getting involved; especially with George's films. George's theatricals are 9/10 documentary, very free-form in some ways. Forty or fifty percent of the shots in DAWN were hand-held, simply because George is such an active director. And there were so many set-ups, and so many locations, and so many instant reactions to scenes that we had to film very quickly, with no chance to really ponder the composition of a shot. But getting back to economics ... When you talk about a 35mm camera, the rent is astronomical. For the box itself, with no lenses or anything else, you're looking at $300 a day. And then there are the lenses. I had to use a lot of super-speed lenses during the mall sequences, because it was impossible to light that damn place at night-I mean, really light it as you would a set. I had to allow for available light, with a spotlight here and there for highlights. I needed a basic complement of four lenses -which ran about $125 a day. Then you have your basic tripods and sound barneys and accessories and on and on-and you find you're very rapidly approaching $1,000 a day.

Despite all reports, we didn't have a million dollars to spend. It was actually closer to $400,000-and that had to cover more than just the basic camera crew. We had logistics expenses-rent-a-cars, helicopters, etc.- and we were watching our budget very carefully.

Now, we did have one other camera. That was the camera which was used to film NIGHT OF THE LIVING DEAD-ten years earlier. We used that as a second-unit camera on really big shots-when we really needed the second angle or where safety was a problem. We had some wild bikers out there, you know. We knew we'd probably only get one take of them. They were so smoked-up and so high that we figured once we opened the doors and got them inside; we'd better film them fast, open the doors again and throw them back out.

What was the main-unit camera?

I used a 35mm Arriflex BL, a German camera which is pooh-poohed by most people. For most feature films, most photographers think in terms of a Panaflex or Panavision camera. In my modest view, I think that most cameras are quite adequate. Beyond that, it becomes a matter of lenses. The BL has a very good internal movement for registering the film.

What I like most is that it's very much like a Volkswagen-very functional and very durable. It's also very light and portable. As I explained before, we did a lot of hand-held stuff, bounding around inside the mall and at the airport. We needed something portable.

It sounds like the perfect commando camera.

Definitely. The BL is used quite frequently in commercial filmmaking, and I think it's just a built-in prejudice of the movie industry in this country to go Panavision.

Backtracking for a moment-you mentioned that the motorcycle shock troops in DAWN were real bikers.

Oh yeah, they were all real. In reality they're all friends of mine, particularly a fellow named Larry, who played the "chief" biker in DAWN. They are actually pretty tender, sensitive guys. I think it's wrong to characterize. all bikers as outrageous barbarians. middle-class Americans go insane in their cars and run each other off the road. guys on bikes, I guess, are just a little more expressive.

On the same topic, George has hinted at the possibility of making a feature film dealing with bikers. Is that being considered?

Yes. The working title is BIKE KNIGHTS *(Editor's Note: This film was eventually made and released as KNIGHTRIDERS),* and hopefully it will be one of our next films. George and I both like the idea very much, but it's still in the treatment staqe. Georqe has always been impressed with medieval chivalry and codes of honor, and he's always wanted to do a Robin Hood or something along that line. One day it simply occurred to us that, in effect, the biker is a modern knight of the road. We Just took it from there and adapted our ideas.

Producers and distributors love the idea, probably because of the success of EASY RIDER and HELL'S ANGELS ON WHEELS. But our film will never be like those. Our intention is to provide a kind of poetic feel for life on the road. In BIKE KNIGHTS, the bikers are a sort of carnival team who earn their living by going around to small towns and performing motorcycle stunts.

Hopefully we'll get a chance to do it. Which were the most difficult scenes to shoot in DAWN?

Probably some of the helicopter approaches, although I'm sure what I went through wasn't any worse than the action other cameramen see. You can't get the true feel from watching the film, but the helicopter generates an amazing gust of wind. I could have shot those sequences from a distance, using a telescopic lens and composing the shots with a zoom. But I chose not to. I was right there, virtually on the landing pad, making hand-held shots with a prime lens. It was incredibly tough to maintain position and composure. And it took a lot of faith in the pilot.

That was physical difficulty, emotionally; I think some of the eating scenes posed the biggest problem. As long as I was composing and working with the camera, everything was fine. It was like watching *CHILLER THEATER*. The most paralyzing moments came afterwards, when I put the camera down and watched some of the zombie extras. They were really immersed in what they were doing, I mean really into it. George would yell "Cut!" and they just couldn't stop. It was more than a little disgusting. We were all a bit squeamish at times, even George. A lot of people picture George as some kind of sadistic idiot. But, even for him, it can get awfully; repulsive on the set.

Despite what the censors or the rating board say, I think there is safety in being a viewer. Psychologists have said that-in the theater-you can cover your eyes, you can go get popcorn, you can look at your neighbor or you can scream. You can escape from the screen in a theater. But when you're working on the set, things can get to be very real. It's all make-believe, sure. But if you're working on any kind of concentrated level, you can get involved almost to the point where it becomes frightening. The early project scenes were like that-when. the SWAT teams were flying through the project, whipping people together and throwing them out of the place. That was a very human moment. The tenants were real people, and they got into the scene. There was a lot of screaming going on, and moaning, and it got frightening.

Sometimes it gets out of hand. You lose control. You think you always have control -but you don't.

Ideally, what is the function of the cinematographer?

On a theatrical film, I would say that the cinematographer should be an expression of the director. Undoubtedly. I think the biggest mistake you can make is to let your ego take over. Filmmaking in general is a committee project, with the committee chairman being the director himself. Everyone offers his or her contribution to the film, but the director channels all those energies into a common focus. There is room for free expression in any kind of a film project, but in the end there has to be a single direction which comes from the leader-who is the director. So I would say that the best approach, the best advice to the cinematographer, is to lay back and be the eyes of the director.

Of course, {here are situations when a cinematographer becomes so well-known or so significant that he is almost on a par above the director. You read little items about DEER HUNTER, for instance, where it's said that Vilmos Zsigmond really directed most of the sequences-that Cimino was actually just a babbling scriptwriter. You wonder how much of that is true. If it is true in a given circumstance, then maybe the titles should be changed. In theory, though, the cinematographer should be the eyes of the director.

Despite the need to accommodate the director's aesthetic sense, do you feel you are developing a cinematic style of your own?

I suppose. Although, again, I believe my style is something which very naturally mirrors George's vision. If you watch TV you will notice a lot of choreographed moves, a lot of wide masters and shots that go on for thirty seconds. In contrast,

George and I have a kind of fragmented style which involves a great number of static shots. We have a lot of action in a scene, but the camera is not required to do incredible moves or pull-backs through windows or dollies or such as that. We are most comfortable with a style which allows us to command a scene within a controlled framework-a literal framework. That is more or less my style.

Would you say that there are any established filmmakers you admire or would like to emulate?

Yes, without a doubt. The most significant filmmaker in my life is Murnau. THE LAST LAUGH had an indelible impression on my life. It may have been an emotional moment in my life, it may have been the storyline-which was beautiful-or it may have been his early style. I don't know. Once I'd seen THE LAST LAUGH, I knew I wanted to immerse myself in film from that point on.

When you compare your own film work to that of mainstream cinematographers, are you comfortable with your own talent?

Oh no. I hate myself. I'm probably my own worst critic. I mean, I absolutely can't stand my stuff. Of course, I have the disadvantage of looking at it every day. I've been involved with DAWN OF THE DEAD for almost a year Now, steadily-so I literally know every element of the film and every last criticism that could be made. I guess it's also a matter of striving to do better. You have to remain highly critical of your own work if you intend to improve it.

It's been said that you put in as much as twenty hours on a single day at the studio. What do you do in your off-hours to break the tension?

Probably watch as little film and TV as I can. I've gotten into a rut where I study things too heavily. Sometimes I find myself turning off the volume on the TV and studying the camera moves. It's terrible.

Basically, I'll do anything that involves a little imagination-imagination, that is, without the eyes.

Tony Buba, Mike Gornick, Tom Dubensky, Marty Schiff and Bob Michelucci together again at a recent screening of George Romero's film MARTIN in celebration of John Amplas' birthday
(Photo by Dawn Michelucci)

LANNY POWERS

GRAPHIC ARTIST

INTERVIEW BY
LEE KARR & CHRIS STAVRAKIS

Conducted MAY 10, 2006 at Café 123, New York

© MAY 2006 by Homepage of the Dead

DAWN OF THE DEAD (1978)

L. L. Powers (informally known as Lanny) is the graphic artist who designed the logo artwork for George Romero's MARTIN and DAWN OF THE DEAD. An accomplished artist who spent a good deal of time in Europe – particularly Spain – Mr. Powers is now curator and exhibition organizer for the Durst Organization, a high-profile Manhattan real estate firm which features contemporary artwork in a number of its midtown properties.

Mr. Powers, how did you come to be involved with DAWN OF THE DEAD?

I had known Richard Rubinstein from Spain – he and his wife had bought paintings of mine, and I had painted a portrait of his wife, as a matter of fact – and when I came to New York, I got in touch with all the people I had known there... Richard said to me, "I'm having trouble getting graphics for this film, would you like to try it?" That was MARTIN. So I went to watch the dailies for MARTIN and the final cut; it was near the end of it, but they still didn't have a graphic, and I came up with what they wanted to use for that...

So the next film was DAWN OF THE DEAD, and he asked me right from the beginning if I would be interested in doing the graphic for that, that's when the zombie head came up. I wondered what I could do that would somehow symbolize the whole thing, and that's what popped up among many sketches that seemed the most appropriate.

What do you recall about the MARTIN assignment?

The whole concept behind that was a simple cutout Valentine heart... there's always a certain amount of love involved in what MARTIN is doing, even though he's fucking them and opening their veins... It's a very perverse film, shocking and yet strangely not, it walks a fine line. I was trying to find something to symbolize that without being too horrific, because it had to be used for subways, all sorts of popular advertising, and that's when that heart thing came up. The heart violated with a razor blade, "MARTIN" done in blood with the big cross... it somehow encapsulated the movie to me.

Please describe how you developed the DAWN logo. Were you given reference photos in addition to viewing dailies?

I watched the dailies, I had photos... I had all sorts of material to work with. The idea came up after doing pages of sketches, just kind of unconsciously doodling. I started thinking, "DAWN, let's see, DAWN..." The thing that symbolizes dawn most of all is the sun coming up over the horizon, and then I thought, "What if it's not the sun, what if it's a zombie head?" Perfect!

How long did it take to design the logo? Did you have any ideas which were initially rejected?

I think it probably took about a week... I wanted the graphic to be a little bit raw, I didn't want it to be too slick... There's a quality to George Romero's work which is very authentic; you sense a kind of calligraphy of the director in it, rather than the glossy façade which most people strive for and is the mark of Hollywood movies. I was trying to come up with a graphic that would have an edge the same way that does, something that felt kind of handmade and a little bit crude so that it had what I felt was the power that was implicit in his approach to filmmaking.

Were you given any sort of instructions or guidelines by Mr. Rubinstein?

Not really, no. That's the way Richard works; the greater the position of responsibility, the less instruction they give you. They don't want to guide you, they want you to surprise them, and they want to see it fresh. They don't want to see a realization of their idea, they want your idea.

How do you feel about the finished work itself? Are you proud of it?

To be honest, I didn't think about it at all for years. What you find is that the things that get remembered that you do in life are often not the things that would have occurred to you that anyone was paying any attention to. This isn't the way the world works, "I'm going to do this, and now everybody will remember that I did this!" No, it was another job and I needed to pay the rent, I was dirt-poor at that time, I had eviction notices for my studio... any job that you could grab was something you grabbed, so I was pleased to have some work.

Did you have any inkling of the pop-culture status that the DAWN logo has attained over the years?

I've heard about it occasionally, but I never took it very much to heart. I mean, if I still had the artwork and I could sell it, that would be something else, but my last rights to that were signed away. It's not something I dwell on.

Was it a profitable assignment?

I made very little. I think I was paid less than $1,000 for doing that.

What media did you use?

I think it was gouache, if I'm not mistaken... but I'm not absolutely positive. I work in so many media.

Does the original painting still exist?

It may, but I don't have it. Richard may have it. About six months ago they asked me for my last rights on that piece because they were selling the rights to the film. Laurel no longer holds the rights to DAWN OF THE DEAD; they sold the entire package and they wanted the graphic as part of the package.

Did you work on any other films for Mr. Rubinstein besides MARTIN and DAWN?

I worked also on DAY OF THE DEAD, the pre-production graphics for that. I didn't do the final take on that. It's not work I'm particularly proud of; I was involved in something else in my life at that time and so I didn't really have the psychic space to devote to getting into that, if you know what I mean. I couldn't sink into it... I had done the other two and it was like, "Oh, another zombie film." This was going to be more of an action movie... it wasn't my bag so much.

You didn't do the final artwork for the one-sheet itself?

Not for DAY, no. I did the pre-production graphics when the package was being put together... sort of the way they envisioned that it would be.

Did you ever have any contact with George Romero himself?

I had contact with him, we sat through the dailies together, we had dinner quite a few times, shared cabs, whatnot. I was never really close with George other than "Hi, how are you?" We were parts of different circles.

How would you describe any differences in personality between Romero and Rubinstein?

You're talking about two completely different worlds. One is the world of a producer, and the other is that of a director. They are not at all the same place; they have not at all the same way of relating to the world... The producer is sort of a position where he's juggling everything, he's concerned with the entire package, sees the image as a commercial application... the total thing, how it's financed, what has to be satisfied...

The director is looking at his expression and satisfying himself, which is the only barometer for the work that he's doing. The aesthetics that are involved in the graphics and whatnot are interesting to him to that degree, but not so much because his real interest is in film. It's in something that involves time, in the sense that time is involved in music. As an art form, cinema involves time, there are rhythms involved... the aesthetic is something that exists in time, the way a symphony does. It's not a painting or a sculpture, which exist outside of time.

What were your impressions of the film itself?

Oh, I quite love the movie.

Were you familiar with the original NIGHT OF THE LIVING DEAD?

Of course. There's a particular quality to the American sensibility which is very exposed in film. There's this kind of... I suppose Walt Disney should be made a saint in some strange way, because the American mind is a rather cartoonish kind of a thing. It creates archetypes, generalized archetypes, and I think George is utterly brilliant in doing that. He has a way of choosing almost absurdist situations that somehow become metaphoric for so many profound issues that you want to discuss in a society, but it happens through that strange American vision which is very different from a European vision or a South American vision... It's a very generalized thing in a way, its texture is very different. It's kind of made of vinyl, in a funny way.

LEONARD
LIES

ACTOR

PERSONAL REFLECTIONS

DAWN OF THE DEAD (1978)

"MACHETE ZOMBIE"

My Love Affair with Zombies and DAWN OF THE DEAD

The first time I did a horror convention was in the year 2000. It was truly a brilliant way to start the new millennium. It started in Ohio near Cleveland when a promoter called me and said, "Hey Len, I'd like you to be a guest at a show featuring actors from DAWN OF THE DEAD?" Quite honestly, I thought it was a scam! Who knew?

My attitude did an about face when I arrived at the convention hotel and walked into the crowded lobby. I could sense 'electricity' in the air. It was something I could taste! As I scanned the room I immediately saw people mingling, hundreds of them, who were from many different continents. I remember feeling excited and thinking, they're here for us! How wonderfully cool! I could never have imagined that DAWN OF THE DEAD would draw so many fans; 22 years later and counting.

When I was a child I wrote stories about monsters. At 12 years old I was a huge fan of NIGHT OF THE LIVING DEAD. I remember watching it and thinking how I'd like to play a zombie, you know, the kind of fantasy you play in your head when you're a kid sitting in the movie theater. At that time, I was a big fan of Famous Monsters of Film Land magazine.

Over time I became fully ensconced in the horror convention milieu it became apparent to me that my childhood dream of becoming a famous monster had arrived! Machete Zombie was quickly putting me in touch with people who I would never have met in my wildest fantasies!

Meeting George Romero:

While attending Point Park University, shooting all the 16mm film I could get my hands on, I read a newspaper article about George Romero's upcoming DAWN OF THE DEAD. The next morning, with resume clutched in hand, I boarded a trolley into downtown Pittsburgh. Holding my breath I entered the building where DAWN's headquarters were located. I went into an open office, but no one was there. Then this tall guy came into frame. I walked up to him, handed over my resume, and started to leave muttering something like, "Will you give my resume to Mr. Romero?" As I turned to go the man said, I'm

George!" and put his hand out to shake mine. I felt like an idiot as I said, "I'm Leonard Lies." He said, "Have a seat and we can talk." Hell yes, I thought!

We talked for about 15 minutes and when I walked out of the office I was walking on air. I felt like I'd really connected with George, who appreciated the fact that I had made and edited several films in 16mm. About two weeks later I was hired as a camera grip and relishing every ecstatic moment.

The Birth of Machete Zombie

Production began in November of 1977 and wrapped in February of 1978. In January of 1978 we were shooting some 3 a.m. set-ups at the Monroeville Mall when we had a brief lull. So I leaned over to George who was quietly pondering the script. I said, "Excuse me George, I'd like to play a zombie." George, being his spontaneous self, said, "Okay man. Go upstairs and see what they have."

The Community room was located upstairs, where actors had make up applied and where crew congregated each night. I literally ran upstairs and talked with the person in extra casting.

I told him that George had given me the green light to see what zombies were available to play. He picked up a machete from a table and handed it to me. I thought, perfect! A groove was cut in the blade to fit onto my head. Twenty-four hours later I'm talking over the scene with Tom Savini.

What happened next!

I'm zombieing through the mall when Tom Savini speeds towards me on a motorcycle. So, I lunge at Tom and knock him 'flying'. He's pissed. He then drop-kicks me to the floor. I sit back up and clutch his leg. Then he pulls a machete out of his boot and says, "Say Good Bye Creep!" He then drives the machete into my skull. The make-up assistant, Jeanie Jeffries, begins pumping a caulking gun with a tube of blood inside of it. And before you know it blood is spewing from my brain. Two different machetes were used for the stunt. When Savini swings the machete, he stops just inches from my head. The camera then stops rolling. Then the blade with the cut in it is placed on my head. When camera begins to roll again Savini pulls the machete out. Using reverse printing and cutting the two shots together it looks like I've bought it.

Here we are 40 years later, and DAWN OF THE DEAD is a hands down classic! The film is revered by its fans around the globe.

People often ask me, would you play another zombie and my answer is, absolutely! It would be fun, and I'd like to experience some of the new make-up that is used in current films.

At this point I'd like to let people know something about my company, Dream Catchers Films, Inc. located in Pittsburgh, PA. I have been an active member of the film industry since 1981. I have established myself as a director, producer, writer, and editor. My background experience includes work on theatrical films, commercials, documentaries, and educational productions.

Since 2012, I have directed and edited three documentary films that were made in Uganda, Africa.

With respect to the horror genre, I'm presently writing a book entitled, 'Diary of a Zombie'. Also, in the works is Zombie Culture, a film I hope to find interviewees for in Manchester during my November 2016 visit.

My Contact info:

Dream Catchers Films, Inc.
3041 West Liberty Ave.
Pittsburgh, PA 15216
412-531-3363
E-mail dreamcatchers@dcfi.co
Web http://dcfi.co
Dream Catchers Films, Inc.

SHARON HILL

ACTRESS, WARDROBE

DAWN OF THE DEAD (1978)

"NURSE ZOMBIE"

I am Sharon Hill and I was the "Nurse Zombie" in the 1978 George Romero film DAWN OF THE DEAD.

Clayton (Hill) and I were in theater at the time that George was putting Dawn together. We ran into Lennie Lies (Machete Zombie) brother, Michael in Pittsburgh and he told us that George Romero was looking for talent for this movie that he is going to be making and we said "OK". What kind of movie was it? He said he wasn't sure but thought that it was some sort of zombie flick.

Well, we went and got our portfolio together and were able to get an interview with George. He liked what we had to say and we liked what he had to say to us. Then he told us that he'd like to feature us in the movie and would we be interested in doing it?

I asked, "do what"? George said that he'd like me to be a zombie and believe it or not, I asked him what a zombie was! George laughed and then just said, well Sharon, I want you to do this and Clayton, I want you to do that...and we said OK, fine. We're in.

After we went home that night, we got a call from George and he asked us if we'd like to work on the film crew too and we told him that we'd love to. He asked me to work wardrobe and Clayton, who already had a firearms background, if he would be the weapons coordinator. And so, we found ourselves both working both in front of and behind the camera on the movie.

Everyone worked together like one big family. We all pitched in and got involved where we were needed.

After the movie had wrapped, Clay and I got booked with a casting company and we both became casting directors for close to twenty years and ended up choosing the talent for several movies.

We moved on to working for several different bands for ten years and then I went and worked for illusionist David Copperfield as his personal assistant for three years.

I made a couple of more movies after that, but it all started from being involved with DAWN OF THE DEAD. I was so fortunate and happy to have been a part of it and to have met so many great fans over the years who are such a huge part of it all.

JOE SHELLEBY

ACTOR

DAWN OF THE DEAD (1978)

"BIKER, LOOTER"

I started in the film business in the early 70's. I did two films for the Lies Brothers, but it would be the next film that I did that would be with me the for next forty years. That movie was the original Romero DAWN OF THE DEAD. I was fortunate enough to have two speaking roles in it as two different characters. I played a Chicano looter named Martinez and I was also a motorcycle raider and I did a couple stunts, too. I was also an assistant for makeup and whatever else that George may have needed me to do. It was such a great pleasure to work with this great director. It was funny that, at the time, I was in awe of Rolling Stone magazine being there when I should've been in awe of the guy directing me. I went on to work on over fifty TV and film projects and I worked with a lot of directors, but Romero has to be at the top. Oh yeah, Gary Zeller, who shot Sonny at the toll booth in THE GODFATHER, was the effects guy that put the squids on my back when I was blown up in the beginning of DAWN!

PART THREE

DAY
OF THE
DEAD

HOWARD SHERMAN

ACTOR

INTERVIEW BY PHIL FASSO

DAY OF THE DEAD (1985)
"BUB"

© Atmosphere Entertainment

For most George Romero fans, myself included, Bub will always be remembered as their favorite zombie. Capable of caring for Dr. Logan, able to shave his face poorly and try to read a book, Bub is a zombie with heart. Fortunately, so is the actor who played him. I met Howard Sherman many years ago, and he was kind enough to discuss Bub and DAY OF THE DEAD.

Let's talk a little bit about Dead. So how did you get the part?

I auditioned. My agents set me up with the auditioned and I went in and did the audition and I got the part. As I recall I figured that eating human flesh would be a substantial role so I brought in a roasted turkey leg and at a strategic point in the audition I whipped out the turkey leg and began devouring get in an appropriate zombie manner and I think that one of the day.

What was it like working for George Romero?
Oh, just terrific. He's a beautiful guy. He's a really sweet and gentle man and he gave me some very strategically important direction that led me to the character and that's always appreciated. Most often in my experiences directors know less than the actor does so it's always a pleasure to work with someone who actually helps you.

I understand you have some input in the role as well. Tell me about Beethoven.

Well after we shot the scene George asked me what music I should be listening to and I think there have been some discussion that it might be some kind of rock 'n roll but I was very adamant that I thought you should either be listening to Mahler's 10th Symphony or maybe Beethoven's ninth and George wisely went with Beethoven's ninth.

What was it like behind all of that makeup?

Well the first time that I stood in front of the mirror with the makeup on and sort of wiggled my face around it became evident that foam latex really acts like flesh. It's a remarkable because it actually started to feel like my own face which was very cool. However, it was a pain in the asked because I tend to perspire a lot and where the edge of the mask met my skin was always a problem because those areas would deteriorate. So, between takes I always had a couple of guys working on me constantly trying to bring the quality of my makeup back up to 100%. That got to be a little tedious, but you know that's the job.

Tom (Savini) was another great guy and a lot of fun to work with. He's kind of a wild man and therefore a lot of fun to have on the set because sometimes the filming can get a little tedious

What was it like working with Richard Liberty? Obviously, Dr. Logan and above have a very intimate relationship in the film?

It was a lot of fun. Richard was a great guy. I'm sorry he's no longer among us.

What do you think of Bub as a character? Why do people love Bub?

I think because in that movie they gave me some very interesting things to do that they've never given zombies to do in any other movie. In the laboratory I would just pick things up and explore them. Then it was all about will you remember what this is? What do you do with a book? What do you do with a razor? What do you do with the gun? Now I approach that and tried to make it as real as possible and very very believable starting with the fact that my fingers didn't work very well and that led to very specific detailed behavior. In most zombie movies zombies just sort of lumber around and try to eat people that they don't really have other activities to engage in other than just lumbering around trying to eat people so if all I had to do was lumber around and try and eat people I would've been just as generic as any other zombie but because I had the opportunity to really do some interesting things and because I tried to bring as much reality to it as possible I think that's why it's remembered.

DAY OF THE DEAD did not get a great reception when it first came out, but it seems as though with DVD it has grown in popularity what are your thoughts about that?

I'm glad to see this continuing to attract an audience. That's the great thing about DVDs is that all this work that we've done has a perpetual life that it did the same in the old days that movies had. They had their run and that was it.

Howard Sherman today

JEFF MONAHAN

ACTOR

PERSONAL REFLECTIONS

DAY OF THE DEAD (1985)

HERE'S MY STORY...

Maybe things are different now with everyone making movies, shooting them on cell phones, even having their own professional camera kits, but back when I did DAY OF THE DEAD, actually being in a movie, any movie, was a big deal. And to be in a George Romero zombie movie was a pinnacle that couldn't be topped.

Being a bold kid, when I heard the movie was being made I went directly to 247 Fort Pitt Boulevard. I knew from my investigative research of looking it up in a phone book (in those days people used phone books), that George Romero had his Laurel Entertainment offices there.

I talked to a woman named Barbara and told her that I wanted to be an actor. She shoved some pages at me and told me to read them for her.

I'm sure a rendition of Steel coming from a skinny kid yelling "I'm going to cut you in half with this machine gun, woman!", was somehow less than stellar. But she told me I could be blue and stagger around and that was good enough for me. I figured I'd get to the Steel and Hamlet parts eventually.

I got a call time to show up on set in the middle of the night, and so made my way to Wampum, PA.

I had no idea where it was, and so followed a map (in those days, people used maps because your car wouldn't tell you where to go). It was cold, it was dark, and I was sleepy.

I parked in a dirty lot and went into a long building and someone threw some make-up on me. Afterwards, we waited around for hours in a big room eating potato chips until we were called to the set. I spent the first day doing the blue-stagger.

In the scene, we zombies were down a long passageway in the mine, trying to make it to Lori Cardille and her friends who had just been forced into the passage by Steel (my lost part), and his military gang.

We were supposed to stagger to them as quickly as possible, so we could eat them. I staggered to them as quickly as possible because the camera was near them and I figured the faster I got there, the sooner I'd be seen.

I enjoyed the process very much, and Barbara asked me if I'd like to come again.

I figured that I was getting paid a dollar a day to freeze in a mine and told her I'd love to. I was having so much fun; I would have paid them a dollar a day.

So I came again another day.

This time, I was ushered into the big make-up room.

I learned that when you got beyond being a blue zombie, there were two more steps up you could go.

Level-twos, who were closer to camera, had masks, and these masks were all over the walls.

I wondered if I was going to be one of these, but then they asked me if I would be a level-one zombie. This was the best kind to be because they weren't just blue, or even masked, but they actually had full make-up jobs.

I said yes, and was introduced to the guy who would do my make-up, Howard Berger.

I spent two and a half hours in the chair while Howard, a really nice and funny guy, made me up. The first application was a small explosive charge attached to my forehead. This would be triggered electronically to explode when I was "shot", and blow through the second application, a latex appliance that gave me a false forehead and made my eyes look all sunken in.

Howard was working with someone, it may have been Greg Nicotero, and as they were applying color, they started a very soft and quiet conversation, muttering to each other and becoming increasingly concerned that something was wrong.

It was early, and I was half asleep, but I realized after a while that they were talking about me.

Howard was worried that he'd placed the explosive, which was filled with gun powder, facing the wrong way. If this was the case, when triggered, the charge wouldn't blow my false forehead out; it would blow my real forehead in. I'd been half asleep but woke up quickly and listened to them discussing the possibility of removing the make-up to check but then deciding against it because it was probably all right.

When I asked if it might not be a good idea to make sure, they both laughed, and I realized that they'd been joking the whole time, just to see my reaction. These movie people were pretty funny.

Howard kept at the make-up and the coloration and decided to create a memorable character with me. He wanted me to have been in the water, and to be all moldy and green. He sent someone out to gather lichen from around the building to glue to my face and clothes.

The longer he worked, the more people started noticing the progress my zombie was making. Chris Romero stopped by and called me Broccoli Man. This was a grand compliment.

Howard kept at it, creating what was, to me, a masterpiece of zombie make-up. He loved it and wanted to have some photos taken. They took some shots of me and of Howard and me together. He told me he'd send me some copies when he got back to Los Angeles. (In those days, you had to have pictures developed).

I wasn't a cynic, but I truly didn't believe that this fantastic artist would take the time to send this kid from Pennsylvania copies of the photos. But several weeks later, I got an envelope in the mail from him. Inside were the pictures and a note from Howard telling me it was his favorite make-up job he'd done on the show. I was thrilled for the pictures, and for having Howard think enough of me to send them.

The scene I was in had me in a doorway as Steel pointed his gun at Bub, who was silhouetted on the other side of a shaded window. I was to jump out and grab Steel. I couldn't see where he was because there was a doorway between us, and because by this time in the day, my prosthetic brow had risen, making my eyes sink in really far.

No problem. George Romero told me he'd shove me through the doorway himself. Action was called, and he threw me. I saw Steel, did the action, which was to grab at him, and miss, coming away only with his hat. It worked.

Then we reversed, and I was to walk to the camera, supposedly to Steel, along with several other zombies. Steel was to shoot all of us.

The other two zombies were blue girls and they were rigged with air-hits. These were tubes to shoot blow out small holes in their foreheads. One of them saw also squibbed in the back of the head like me.

So, here I was with an explosive charge at my forehead and a condom filled with blood on the back of my head, both rigged to go off simultaneously, a bullet hole appearing at the front of the head while the back of the head exploded in a shower of blood.

You get one take at a gag like this, so I wanted to do it right. But how do you do it right if you've never been shot in the head before?

Worse, how do you do it right when your false face is swelling forward so far that you're blind?

I'd love to tell you, but I don't really remember. All I know is that I went towards camera, they blew the explosives and I staggered away, dead and bleeding. It was one of the most exhilarating things I'd ever done.

Afterwards, I drove home on the PA turnpike. The appliances had been removed, but half of my face was still mottled and green, my hair was plastered to my scalp, and dried blood was caked my neck. I stopped and paid my toll. No one noticed... just another zombie.

I've since done other films with George, but the memories of those days in the mine will last the rest of my life. And memories of being a zombie... maybe even longer.

BARBARA RUSSELL

ACTOR

PERSONAL REFLECTIONS

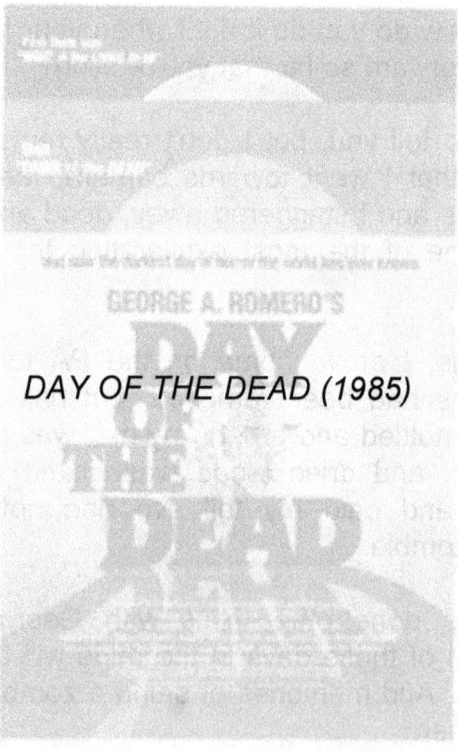

DAY OF THE DEAD (1985)

© Atmosphere Entertainment.

My memory of being on set is that I spent more time in make-up than I did on the set. I was a beauty parlor zombie...I had a hair dryer plastic cap on with the hose still attached. I never visit anyone in the hospital that has tubes attached, is moaning or is the color grey.... I will faint. So, when I was watching my face being turned into someone who got hit across the eyes with a baseball bat and had open sores on my neck I began to get lightheaded. I of course, did not tell the make-up guy that I was a wimp...I just blamed it on the glue that was being used for the prosthesis. I went to the Ladies' Room and stared at the mirror long enough to get used to my new look and then returned for more make up.

When I did get to the set for my first shot, George Romero said my arms looked too nice (I was wearing a short-sleeved dress) so it was back to make-up to have my arms painted with some substance that caused the skin to wrinkle... it took two hours every night to peel it off! My role was to bite off the neck of an actor. What fascinated me was the amount of detail that was taken for everything to be anatomically correct.... even to inserting hairs in the prosthesis to look like the fellow hadn't shaved. I was to chew on a piece of his neck after the bite...I was given a piece of Spam...I think I would have rather chewed the neck!

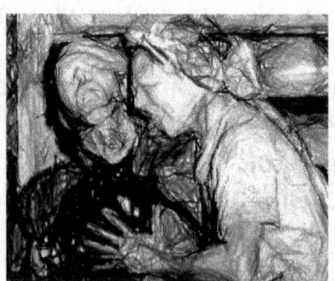

© Atmosphere Entertainment.

LORI CARDILLE

ACTOR

PERSONAL REFLECTIONS
MY FATHER "CHILLY BILLY"

DAY OF THE DEAD (1985)

© Atmosphere Entertainment.

MY FATHER "CHILLY BILLY"

When George Romero had the opening of his film LAND OF THE DEAD in Pittsburgh, the theater was jammed. In the audience were Quentin Tarantino, Robert Rodriguez and Simon Pegg to name a few.

George got up on the stage before the film began and thanked my father for his career. You see, my father was Bill Cardille, "Chilly Billy," host of the most popular show in Pittsburgh for over 20 years, CHILLER THEATER He was one of the first horror hosts in the country, a pioneer of early television. He signed on the NBC affiliate here in the 'burgh, WIIC. He was Pittsburgh's beloved hero, a Pittsburgh icon turned legend.

In 1968, Chilly Billy was talking to his large Chiller audience about this little movie he just made with George Romero called, NIGHT OF THE LIVING DEAD™. He played himself, Bill Cardille, cool, calm and collected, in control of the airwaves, reporting about this new phenomenon, *The Walking Dead*, of course now known as ZOMBIES!!!!!

Because Chilly/daddy was so popular and trusting, people knew they had to go see this new film he kept plugging on Chiller about the dead coming back to life and eating people.

"CHILLY BILLY" Cardille, Lori's father in NIGHT
(Photo courtesy Bob Michelucci)

Author Bob Michelucci on the Chiller Theater set with Bill Cardille
(Photo by Charles Edwards)

"Chilly Billy" on the set of Chiller Theater   (Photo by Charles Edwards)

I remember going to the premier of NIGHT OF THE LIVING DEAD™. I was in the eighth grade. I was terrified to watch the movies on dad's show. I couldn't understand why people liked to be terrified. It sure wasn't fun for me. I was so afraid watching the premiere of this new film that I spent the entire movie in the lobby.

Years later, while working as an actress in New York, zombies came back into my life. I was doing a new play called RECKLESS by Craig Lucas. My character's name was Rachael and I was on stage the entire play. She was this wonderful character who ruled the stage. One evening, George Romero was in the audience. He offered me a part in a new movie he was writing called DAY OF THE DEAD. The rest is George Romero zombie history.

Lori in DAY OF THE DEAD (Photo courtesy Lori Cardille © Atmosphere Entertainment.)

My father, Chilly Billy, is my hero. Thank you, daddy. I love you.

Bill,Sr., Lori, Maria and Billy

Here's another little interesting bit of trivia. Did you know that my brother Billy played the "Soldier Zombie" going down the elevator in DAY? He was going to a Halloween party that evening and kept his makeup on. We had to call Tom (Savini) when he couldn't get it off. His face was a raw mess. Hahahahaha. There was another actor (sorry, I don't know his name) who played it in Florida. He was one of the Zombies on the elevator eating Miguel. Be well everyone. Thanks for being such great fans!!!!

JOE PILATO

ACTOR

© April 2000 by Homepage of the Dead

DAY OF THE DEAD (1985)

© Atmosphere Entertainment.

How and why did you get into acting? Was it a goal or did you fall into it?

I always thought when I played as a little kid that I played better than the other kids. Like when we played army and stuff the other kids didn't die right, and I always died like Vic Morrow on TV or something like that. Then I became an altar boy when I went to school, Catholic school, and I kinda really enjoyed being on stage, which was the alter as an altar boy. And then I kinda forgot about it, nothing happened through high school or anything like that and I had aspirations of going to law school.

When I was in college in my freshman year I was involved in a production in a technical capacity doing lights and working back-stage and then I started taking some acting classes and played the role of Tom in *The Glass Menagerie* - This was in the 70's, late 60's, the avant-garde days of theatre - So I quit college and joined a troop, studying, taking different workshops and toured Europe with the Stage One Theatre company. I came back and stayed in experimental theatre until I moved to Pittsburgh to study more and that's how the film thing started. I made a film called EFFECTS (1978) with Tom Savini and John Harrison which never got distributed.

So that was your first film?

I had done something for television, but EFFECTS was the first shot!

How did you actually get involved in that? Was it sheer luck? Did you know someone?

I was working for a theatre company and I had to give a girl a ride over to the audition and I had been out of town so I hadn't heard about it and I was all pissed off because everybody I knew was auditioning, except for me! So I drove the girl over and they needed someone to read with her, so I read and she ended up not getting the part, and they ended up re-writing the whole lead character for me.

So that was your lucky break?

Well, it would have been a luckier break if the film went somewhere! But yeah, I got paid, bought a car and it was a good deal and I enjoyed it immensely.

Then the next big step was getting involved with DAWN OD THE DEAD (1978)?

Yeah! In fact, I was broke, had no money and had to call my folks to wire me money to get a wardrobe to fly to New York 'cause they were reading me for the helicopter pilot.

Really? I didn't know that!

Oh yeah! I have a lot of fucking hit and misses here pal! <Laughs> But I was too similar in type to Scotty so they went with David. It was a look thing! So they flew me up to New York and read and I didn't get it. I came back, but then George was kind enough to cast me on the dock as the renegade cop and I had some fun.

After that I kinda stuck around Pittsburgh and he threw me a nice little bone with KNIGHTRIDERS (1981). I got to work with Ed Harris which was real nice. I had auditioned for a bigger part but I couldn't ride a bike so that didn't help.

So with KNIGHTRIDERS did George think directly of you, or was there an audition again?

You have to remember Pittsburgh was such a small town that everybody knew everybody. So, when anything was happening everyone knew! Everybody usually came in because the acting pool was very small. So you were always in there.

From what I've heard, Romero looks upon KNIGHTRIDERS as one of his favorite projects?

I think that and MARTIN, yeah! I think had he had more money for MARTIN it could have really been a great film. I mean it's a film great anyway, but it could have been much better I think.

Leading into DAY OF THE DEAD, did George think of you for a role in that film?

He pretty much just gave it to me. I don't know if he

auditioned other people, but it was very quick. I came in and it was like, "You got it!"

It almost sounds like he had you in mind?

Well, I don't know... The original story he wanted to do was a lot different to the one that got done.

I've read the original script and I'd almost say Rhodes was the only character to truly make it to the final film. You know, I was the only actor never to go to Florida, so I was upset! I tried to convince George that when they we were digging Major Cooper's grave that I should be out there supervising! So I didn't get to go to Florida in the middle of winter.

You must get asked about your death scene a lot. You actually ad-libbed the final line?

I can remember it like it was yesterday. I had been thinking about it and I can remember thinking Rhodes is not the kind of guy to take this lying down, no pun intended! <Laughs> I got to the set that day and said, "Hey George, can I talk to you?" and he said, "Yeah, what's up?" I said, "Look, I think Rhodes would say something!" And he said, "Well what?" So I whispered in his ear "Choke on 'em!" and he just laughed and he said, "You got it!"

The prep on that was amazing! It was like three hours and they had two cameras rolling and because of the low budget they said, "We're not going again! We're getting it or we're not!" So, if I messed up with the line it would have sucked. But it worked, and I think it's a pretty strong cinema death.

How bad were those three hours?

Oh, it was like an astronaut getting into a capsule, with the hole and me getting in there. I was exhausted!

Can you tell me more about the infamous guts that had gone off over night?

The smell was just horrible, horrendous, and horrible! I was on a ventilator until the shot because the smell was so bad! They put them in the fake torso and covered them up and the smell kinda went away, but when the zombies started tearing it apart and I didn't have the ventilator on, as soon as they had cut I was just laying there gagging! It was fun! <Laughs>

Obviously the films we've mentioned so far are small Independent productions, but you've also been involved in larger Hollywood films.

You know originally FROM DUSK TILL DAWN was written for me? But it didn't happen... It happened for George Clooney! It had to be about '88 and I got a call from Bob Kurtzman and he wanted me to read the script and write a letter of intent. So I went to a party and there was Quentin and he was like, "Oh wow! Captain Rhodes!" Anyway, months go by nothing, nothing, nothing! Then one day I wake up and two words RESEVOIR DOGS were all over the place. Apparently, he had taken the money from writing Dusk to start up RESEVOIR DOGS. So, the next thing you know Quentin is like the next Orson Welles. Still Dusk can't get made. From what I understand Kurtzman was trying to unload it. The next thing you know Quentin buys it back and makes it and I didn't even get an audition! <Laughs> It's a sad story! I was in the original trailer. Maybe I should put that out on the website and sell it for like ten bucks a copy? <Laughs> there's me, before RESEVOIR DOGS came out, in the black suit with the white shirt and black tie, the whole Tarantino thing!

Do you do many conventions?

About a year and half ago they had a reunion of the DAY OF THE DEAD cast at Fangoria in New York. We were on stage for an hour and there must have been a thousand people in the hall, and we were at the autograph table for like three and a half hours. The fans were just great. I don't do as many as I'd like to, but I get a call occasionally to go, and it's always fun. The fans are real fans! They're down to earth, they're great, and they're fun people.

In-between films, what can you be found doing?

I like to golf. I play the trombone, which I taught myself - my father was a professional musician - and I play the guitar and accordion.

What's George like to work with?

Oh great! The image I have of George is being in a hotel, waking up at 6:00 a.m., looking out the window at a snowy dreary Pennsylvania day and there's George scrapping off the windshield to his car, no driver, going to the set, driving himself. He's just a great panda bear kinda guy! (Laughs)

GLEN CHARBONNEAU

ACTOR

PERSONAL REFLECTIONS

DAY OF THE DEAD (1985)
"ZOMBIE"

Back in the mid '80s, "Midnight Madness" was a popular weekend pastime for us in our late teens. Local movie theaters would show all kinds of "cult classic" movies like Eraserhead, The Song Remains the Same, The Wall, Rocky Horror Picture Show etc., but my favorite was always "DAWN OF THE DEAD", by George Romero. My friends and I would go see it quite often, and heckle the screen the entire time...... After a semester at Hofstra, commuting from home, trying to maintain a music scholarship, college work and learning to fly on the side, I decided, with the help of my parents, that I needed to focus on one thing or the other, so I chose flying.

I ended up transferring to a small community college (Community College of Beaver County) north of Pittsburgh that had a great degree program centered on flying. George Romero lived and did a bulk of his filming the in the Pittsburgh area, so one of the first things I did when I moved to the area was to visit the Monroeville Mall, where DAWN OF THE DEAD was filmed. In early '84, it still looked exactly like it did in the movie. To my dismay, the gun shop was not in the mall. That was made up for the movie. Unfortunately, I didn't even own a camera, so no pics! They were just dismantling the ice skating rink when I was there.

One day, during the fall of '84, I was sitting in instrument class, and I overheard the girl in front of me say "Can you believe he wanted me to be a ZOMBIE?" Being the New Yorker I am, I butted in and asked: Is George Romero making another movie? She answered "yeah!" It turned out that she knew him somehow (neighbor, babysitter or something like that). I pleaded with her to get me any info about casting.

DAY OF THE DEAD

NAME	PHONE #	Time	SIGNED IN	SIGNED OUT	coming back?	
19.) Burgess, Jeffrey	885-5756	7:45		69	JB	L
20.) Burkholder, Les	264-2493 355-7109(w)	X 7:30		1	JB	L
21.) Cable, Kevin	392-3203(w) 257-1596(w)	X 7:45		53	KC	L
22.) Caputo, Frank		X 7:45		51	FMC	L
23.) Caputo, JoAnne I		X 7:45		50	JC	L
24.) Caputo, JoAnne II		X 7:45		34	JC	L
25.) Caputo, Mary		X 7:45		30	MC	L
26.) Yardille, Billy	367-4303	X 8:30				—
27.) Carroll, Charles		X 7:30				—
28.) Cassidy, Gordon	337-7469	X 8:30		78	CO	V
29.) Cassidy, John	231-0915	X 9:45		13	JC	L
30.) Charbonneau, Glenn	847-2739	X 8:15		102 ✓	MC	L
31.) Clemens, Ron	523-5254	X 7:45		95	RC	V
32.) Clinton, Zill ©		X 7:30				—
33.) Colarusso, Mike	422-0213	X 7:45		41	MC	N
34.) Collelo, John	823-3834	X 7:30		40	JC	L
★ 35.) Clifton, Joan	766-9525	8:17		61	JC	L
36.) Coriga, Paul	433-3954	X 8:10				—

Scan of DAY IF THE DEAD sign-in sheet; I believe the "102" signified either the mask or costume issued to me and the check indicates I returned it. (Photo courtesy Lee Karr and Greg Nicotero)

A few days later, she gave me the number for the casting office, which was located in Wampum PA, a few towns north of where I lived in Beaver Falls! I called them, and they said that they were still casting extras, and to come to the office and fill out the release forms. My roommate Wayne and I went up there that day, walked in and said: We want to be

Zombies! The casting lady laughed, and said "type casting, huh?" We filled out standard release forms and another form with our height, weight, measurements etc. She said they'd call if they needed us.

I went home and immediately called Steve Mellis, and told him to rally the midnight madness troops, and make a road trip out to be in the movie. After some initial enthusiasm, nothing ever came of that idea!

A few days after we visited the casting office, the casting people called and asked us if we were available on November 4th 1984, and we both said YES! We had to go back to the casting office to get the info package, which included directions to the site, some kind of "invitation" that would let us get on the set and instructions to wear old shoes.

As an aside, the casting offices were actually located in the interior sets seen throughout the movie. We didn't know it at the time of course but casting and admin offices were actually the sets for the "lab scenes". I drank from the water fountain seen in the hallway. All of this was located in a neat place called the "Wampum Mine", which was, at some point, an actual mine. At the time of filming, most of it was underground commercial storage, which is why you see motor homes, boats, etc. in a lot of the scenes during the movie.

The scene I was in was filmed at a decommissioned NIKE missile base located in Manor PA, not far from the Monroeville Mall. Wayne and I arrived at 7:30 a.m. for the filming. There were a ton of people there already! It was also really cold out, being early November in Pittsburgh...

We reported to the "extras" area and were issued a really cool zombie mask and our "costume". Wayne got to be soldier, and I got to be "artist", or that's what I think it was. Corduroy pants and jacket and a beret... Totally lame, but hey, it's all part of "the business", and being the professional that I am, started to get dressed. As soon as I started pulling my pants on, I knew there was a problem... Back in the casting office, they made us put our measurements on the release form, to ensure that our costumes would fit... I had a 32 waist at the time, wrote that down, yet the pants I was issued were 28 at best. No amount of sucking in would result in being able to get these things buttoned, so I asked the costume guy if it was possible to just wear my jeans. He would have none of that, and took a huge pair of scissors and cut the pants from the nether region up the back, and then tied it all up with a piece of twine! Good thing I wore "clean" (which is a relative term in college!) underwear, as they were hanging in the breeze all day!

After the costumes were done, they put a little eye makeup on us, because that's all you'd be able to see when wearing the mask. They also painted our shoes to make them look old (mine already were!), and then sent us on our way. I got to meet George Romero, Tom Savini and Lori Cardille (although at the time, I didn't know who she was) and several of the other "real" actors in the film. They filmed us all day, going up and down the large elevator that was formerly used to move the missiles from the underground storage magazine and maintenance areas to the surface. They only used about 3 seconds of that in the finished cut. It's the scene near the end where the wimpy soldier Miguel, lets the zombies into the complex. I am on the left side of the screen somewhere, in the group of about 50 zombies. I have gone through the DVD frame by frame, and can't make out which one is me, but I can see my roommate Wayne as one of the soldier zombies. He's the shorter of the 2. The "kid" in the football uniform was actually a rather attractive blonde girl!

After the filming, they gave us all a boxed lunch (cold fried chicken), a dollar bill signed by Tom Savini (a fact that I didn't know until after I spent it at Wendy's on the way home!) and a painter's cap that said "I WAS A ZOMBIE IN DAY OF THE DEAD", which also disappeared somewhere along the line...

Before they let us leave, we had to surrender our costumes, including the mask (that I desperately wanted to keep!). They wouldn't give us our clothes back until they checked us off a list as having returned our stuff... If my wallet wasn't in my jeans, I would've sacrificed my clothes to keep the costume!

Wayne and I went back home and warmed up... We both agreed that it was a great day!

When the movie was released in the summer of '85, all of my friends and I went to the Sunrise Mall to see the movie. Before it began, Steve Mellis stood up on his seat and yelled: "EXCUSE ME EVERYONE... I HAVE AN ANNOUNCEMENT! MY FRIEND, GLENN CHARBONNEAU WAS A ZOMBIE IN THIS MOVIE!" Which was met with a few "shut the f*** ups and various catcalls....I was mortified... but even more mortified that I couldn't see myself! I've since pored over every print of the movie that can get my hands on, and no go. The only explanation I can come up with is that the take used in the movie was one of the ones where my roommate and I stayed up top, at ground level, instead of riding the elevator down. We did this, ironically, because we were always near the back of the crowd and wanted to be seen. There were several cameras filming the action looking down at the elevator from topside, and we made sure to stand right in front of them. I assume that they didn't use any of this topside footage due to continuity, as the film takes place in SW FL, and November in the Pittsburgh area looks nothing like Sanibel Island, where the rest of the topside scenes were filmed.

My wife Donna (girlfriend at the time!) spent the entire movie looking at the inside of her hand...

So, that's how I came to be a zombie in DAY OF THE DEAD!

PART FOUR

LAND OF THE DEAD

DIARY OF THE DEAD

GREG NICOTERO

MAKE-UP ARTIST, SPFX, PRODUCER, DIRECTOR

**INTERVIEWS BY NEIL FAWCETT
& LEE KARR**
© June 2005, December 2006 by
Homepage of the Dead

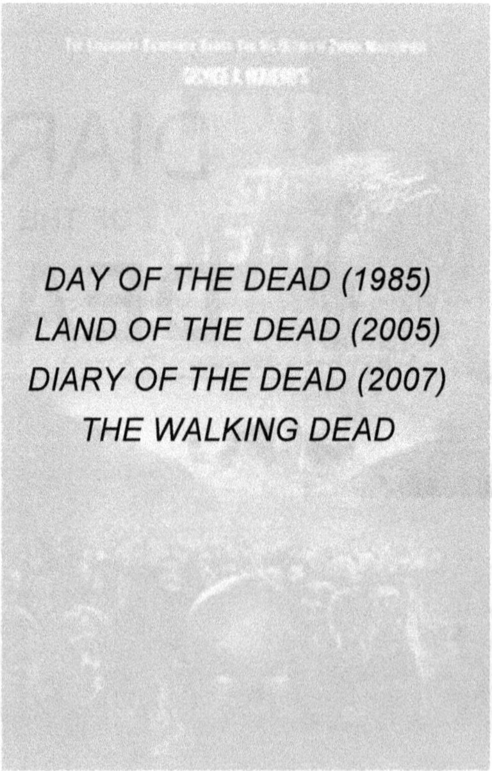

DAY OF THE DEAD (1985)
LAND OF THE DEAD (2005)
DIARY OF THE DEAD (2007)
THE WALKING DEAD

LAND OF THE DEAD

Your first involvement with Romero was on DAY OF THE DEAD while you were still at college. How did you manage to not only get involved on that project, but also on both sides of the camera (makeup & acting)?

Having grown up in Pittsburgh, if you have any interest in the film community or movies in general then you are likely to run into George Romero. Given that fact, I was fortunate enough to befriend George and Christine through an association with Sam Nicotero (my uncle) who is not only a Pittsburgh actor who had a part in THE CRAZIES but wrote for Cinefantastique on NIGHT and was a disc jockey.

My friendship with Tom Savini developed on my visits to the set of CREEPSHOW and low and behold a few years later I was offered a job on DAY OF THE DEAD by George and Chris. The first thing I did was pick up the phone and call Tom and say "I just got hired on DAY...can I be your assistant". The rest, as they say, is history. 20 years and 500 movies later I find myself standing next to George looking at 200 zombies on a freezing cold night in Toronto, Canada.

There were many extremely gory scenes in DAY, did you ever wonder 'My God! What have I got myself into here?

Never...I still think DAWN OF THE DEAD is one of the greatest horror movies ever made... My top 10 list hits JAWS, Carpenter's THE THING among others...but DAWN really affected me.

Does it seem odd that twenty years later here you are doing another Romero Living Dead movie? Did you ever think that this fourth film would never see the light of day?

George and I had been talking about this film since 2002... He sent the first draft over and I budgeted the effects for him...allowing for the 'Pittsburgh' discount of course (given the fact that he is the guy that started my career). With the superb 28 DAYS LATER (not really a zombie movie but ripped off) the remake of the DAWN and RESIDENT EVIL movies and the brilliant SHAUN OF THE DEAD...it without a doubt laid the groundwork for this film.

Did you ever think that this fourth film would never see the light of day?

2 years, 20 years, 200 years...there will always be people clamoring for a Romero zombie movie!

In DAWN OF THE DEAD the zombies were the traditional blue grey. In DAY they were more grotesque and aged, and in the NIGHT remake

more akin to a fresh cadaver. **Is there a particular style/theme to the makeup of the creatures in LAND?**

Given the great work on all those films...we wanted to try a few different things to give the make-ups some character. Custom dentures, eyebrows, contact lenses in every hero zombie...a yellowish base with purples to accent...that kind of thing. We ended up doing on average 30 zombies a night, then with background masks we could provide over 120 zombies...and they were all used! I wanted to stay away from building the brows up too much because people end up looking Neanderthal...and the teeth were grey-ish black...

We also made up about 20 "sparse" hair wigs that we used either on bald actors or people that we put partial bald caps on so that you had zombies that looked like the hair had been falling out...a pretty effective technique.

Were there any particular hurdles LAND offered regarding effects? For example, in the trailers and stills we can see zombies emerging from water – I would imagine water and makeup are not the best of friends!

Well, George spent almost the entire prep of the film re-writing and finessing the script. I think the biggest challenge was the shooting schedule itself. DAY 1 – 150 ZOMBIES IN THE WATER...DAY 2 150 ZOMBIES IN THE WATER...and it never let up.

We did a 60-day shoot in 40 days...and with that said every night we were in a different location. It wasn't like the Monroeville Mall or Wampum Mine where everything was basically lit and we were in the same place for weeks...there was a story to be told...then we'd get around to the gags at the end of the night...it's always better to have lots of time to finesse the effects, do multiple takes to insure that you get on film exactly what you want...and we didn't have that luxury here because we had so much to shoot every night just to get the coverage to cut the scenes together.

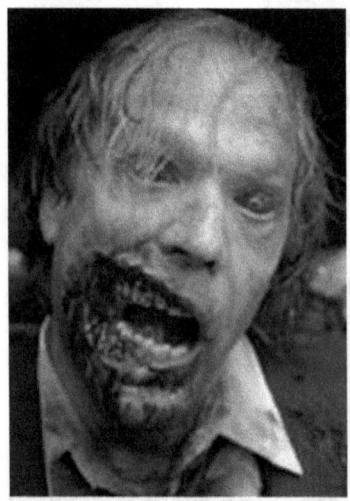

(Photo courtesy Homepage of the Dead)

What sort of quantity of makeup/effects artists were involved on an average day of shooting? I assume on some days there was quite a production line required?

I would say most of the time we had 14 people...5 guys from KNB here in LA and the rest from Toronto. I had a great bunch of guys...the US crew consisted of Gino Crognale, Alex Diaz, Jake McKinnon and Chris Nelson while the Canadian guys (many who worked on the DAWN remake) ranged from Sean Sansom, Francois Dejeunese, Kyle Glencross, Damon Bishop, Patrick Baxter, Tracy Loader, Anthony Vieuxilleu, CJ Goldman, Alan Cross, Tara Murphy, Pam Hackwell (Hope I didn't leave anyone off) ... and it was tough. We'd start at 3:00 in the afternoon, shoot from 8 til 6:00......then clean up and get back to the hotel by 9:00...go to bed and hit it all over again.

How long could the makeup take to be applied?

We tried to keep each make-up to an hour and a half...

When working on such a project, can the script change due to input from the effects team? For example, the script may specify something that is simply too difficult or not cost effective? Or the effects team may have a different/alternative idea on a scene?

Some of the ideas that ended up in the script came from sketches or things we threw at George...he's the kind of guy that rarely says "no"...but it did come down to time. There were a few gags that were designed to have some visual effects elements...mainly to keep the audiences on their toes and not let them get too comfortable with what they were going to see.

It would have been fun to brainstorm a bunch of stuff on the fly...but we didn't get a chance to do a lot of that (even though one of the most effective gags was done on the spur of the moment the last night of shooting).

Sometime ago there was talk of effects involving 'full body zombies' or 'mechanical zombies'. Were these sorts of effects/techniques used in the end?

I really wanted to use some puppet heads of extremely rotted zombies just to show that some of these things have been around for a long time. There are a few puppet shots that I think look great...so I'm hopeful that audiences and fans will agree.

In this modern era where CGI is encroaching more and more into films, what part has it played on LAND?

I have always felt that cgi work is a great tool...when used to further practical elements or help tell the story in a subtle way. SPIN (the Canadian visual effects company) has done a great job in realizing a lot of the gags as I had imagined them...and the augmentation on the crowd shots is amazing!!!!

Was there ever the possibility of you stepping in front of the camera in LAND for a small part/role?

Very much like DAY OF THE DEAD, I was able to cast a few of the KNB guys in key zombie roles that required not only special make-up but gags (radio-controlled heads, puppet work), so Alex, Gino, Chris and myself all have featured zombie roles... Of course with us it is always easier to have an effects guy execute a gag to insure that it is 'pulled off' as intended.

Are you aware if there will be a stronger (unrated) version of the film released later (on DVD)?

Without a doubt. People need to remember that contractually the film is going to be rated R - the first mainstream release of a Romero zombie movie ever - so ratings play a part. But rest assured the DVD will not only have some great gags...but I have turned over hours of my personal behind the scenes footage (similar to what I shot for Tom on DAY) so that fans can see first-hand the creation of the effects.

Are there any rumblings about a fifth installment? If so, will we have to wait twenty years again?

I'm sure if plenty of people plop down there cash to see this in the theatres and it does well...people will consider another...but I have no actual knowledge as of yet. Given all of the films KNB has been involved with, from SIN CITY, KILL BILL and THE CHRONICLES OF NARNIA, my ultimate hope is that George has a hit on his hands. Anyone that has ever worked with him puts 150% effort in to ensure that *HIS* movie is well done and hopefully well received.

(Photo courtesy Lee Karr)

DIARY OF THE DEAD By Lee Karr:

Greg, what is your role this time around on DIARY OF THE DEAD?

Well, this production came up pretty fast. I got a phone call from Peter Grunwald and John Harrison saying that George wanted to do another zombie film, very different from what George is used to doing. He wanted to get back to his roots where it was a smaller, manageable crew and a smaller production, but gave him a little more freedom to be as creative as he wanted to be. So, their plan was to have a four week prep and a four week shoot which is pretty crazy and pretty unheard of, considering the fact that most movies shoot for ten, to twelve, to fourteen weeks, depending on the film.

We (KNB EFX) were in the middle of about six other projects at the time; we were doing GRINDHOUSE, HILLS HAVE EYES 2, TRANSFORMERS, MASTERS OF HORROR, PRINCE CASPIEN...we were really, really busy. So, there was some question as to whether or not we would be able to be involved or how involved we could be.

Now, George and Peter both wanted me involved in the project and I wanted to be involved. I've had a loyalty to George for 22 years, so as far as I was concerned I would be willing to contribute in any capacity. So, they came up with a pretty good, mutually beneficial plan, which was we would design the look of the zombies and consult on a lot of the gags. Then I would basically hand pick a crew in Toronto that would execute the effects. A couple of names came up, all of whom I had worked with before. A lot of the guys that were on LAND OF THE DEAD, on my crew, had branched out to start their own effects companies, Francois Dagenais and Kyle Glencross. I knew all of them and I knew that they all had different talents, and all were probably up to the challenge. Kyle (Glencross), Chris Bridges, and Neil Morrill started a company called Gas Light Studios in Toronto. They were looking for their first break, their first show that could put them on the map. So I thought they were a perfect choice for the show because they were enthusiastic, talented, and I knew that they would go that extra mile because they were working on a George Romero zombie movie, which is really every effects guy's dream.

So we (KNB EFX) came up with the basic design of the zombie makeups and I had some ideas that were inspired by some older films and some things that I just wanted to try to make them look different. My standard thing is that I always want stuff to look different. I don't want to ever see a movie and feel like 'Oh, we've seen those zombies before...we've seen those characters before', I always want to change stuff up. We came up with some pretty unique concepts that hadn't been done before. And I'm really proud of them because they are really pretty outlandish when you think about it, but very simple.

So, we ended up consulting with the guys and they built all the effects. I thought they did a tremendous job. They had no time to do the effects and it was a limited budget. I was really impressed with them and I think they've got great careers ahead of them. So, I was kept in the loop in terms of how the gags were changing and they would call me and ask me what I thought about a gag, basically as a consultant. It was the first time that I had ever really done that, usually I'm much more hands on. It was kind of an interesting scenario, something I'd never done before. I was really putting a lot of my confidence and trust in these other guys. If they screwed up I was going to look like an idiot because I recommended them. It was a little scary, but I had 150% confidence in them because I knew they would do a great job. All in all, everybody was happy. George was really, really pleased and I think they did top notch work.

How much has George's style changed since you first worked for him?

Well, George's style always changes and always matures. The whole concept of this film was developed by John Harrison and George several years ago. I had heard initial talk about this being done as a TV series. The idea was that you're with this group of people, shooting real time, as they come upon the realization that zombies are real. It's certainly a much different prospect than what George has done before, because you are really playing to today's audience. George has never really played to an audience before. He's made the movies that he's wanted to make. This film relies on people's knowledge of the internet and that kind of stuff. It's much more current and I think that's going to appeal to a lot of people.

Can you talk about John Harrison's involvement on the picture?

John and George have always been a great team. I met John on DAY OF THE DEAD and we've had a great relationship. We've (KNB EFX) done a couple of films with John. We worked on his miniseries DUNE for the Sci-Fi channel and subsequently won an Emmy award. He was instrumental in spearheading the idea that we consult on the makeups, because there was a certain comfort level there. John knows my devotion to George and my love of the zombie genre.

Will there be CGI this time around too?

Listen, there's always a requirement for a mix. I've said for a while that we would be utilizing a mixture of puppets, prosthetics, and CGI. A lot of the CGI effects that were designed in LAND OF THE DEAD by me, George, and the guys at Spin (visual efx company) worked really well. They didn't feel digital, they felt seamless. To do a zombie head shot and blow part of his head away or do a blood splatter against a wall, and be able to add that later, instead of shooting that for real...it just makes sense to have the guy react and add the blood spray later. The plan was to always do a lot of that.

In retrospect, looking back at LAND OF THE DEAD, there were certain people who were not quite clear on that when we went into it. I always knew we would need a mix of that to pull those effects off and ultimately, I thought they looked great. I thought LAND OF THE DEAD had a great feel to it and I thought the effects were great. I was really happy them.

What were your thoughts on how Land of the Dead turned out?

I think it's a great movie. I remember the first time George showed it to me, I felt like I was watching a 40-million-dollar film. It looked like a big budget zombie movie.

I took Frank Darabont to a screening in Los Angeles and he loved it! The first thing he said to me was 'Let's get George on the phone right now; I want to tell him how much I liked the movie'. He was really satisfied and very entertained. I was really excited by that because it was a labor of love for me, as well as George. It was a hard project. It was challenging, we shot all nights for 3 months and everybody was tired. It was a rough shoot. But, I thought that the movie was great and I was really proud of what George did and I was proud of the makeup designs that we came up with.

And it was nice to see the reviews and have the reviews talk about what a well-crafted film it was and how creepy and effective the zombie makeups were. That was one of the things that was most important to me, was coming up with some original looking zombies that people didn't feel like they had seen before.

Any words for the loyal fans at "Homepage of the Dead"?

I love Homepage of the Dead! I love the fact that they have such a great devotion to George. He loves making movies for the fans and he really enjoys the fans. It's a great website and I go on it all the time. I'm a zombie fan too!

JOHN HARRISON

EXECUTIVE PRODUCER

INTERVIEW BY LEE KARR

© February 2008 by Homepage of the Dead

DIARY OF THE DEAD (2007)

Most of you probably don't need an introduction to John Harrison. If you are a fan of George Romero, and you are on this site, then you already know all about him and his place in the Romero family tree. And if you don't, then you should have a screwdriver shoved in your ear!

Mr. Harrison was nice enough to take time out from editing his latest film, BOOK OF BLOOD for Clive Barker, to talk about his involvement with George Romero's newest zombie project.

The obvious first question is, how did you come to be involved with DIARY OF THE DEAD?

Well over the past 5 years, more maybe, George and I and his partner Peter Grunwald have been talking about trying to do some television, trying to get some ideas done. We've had a couple of false starts at different places. George had this idea at one point - you know those frustrating days we all have when nothing is going on and we can't get anything off the ground - "you know man, I'm just gonna go down to the film school and I'm gonna get a bunch of kids together and I'm gonna go back to my roots and I'm just gonna shoot a film on video". He had this idea, which I always loved, and I thought maybe it could in fact be a cool TV. series or a web series, because that was all starting to happen. That was the origin of DIARY.

What you see now in the movie was always the general idea of what he had in mind. So the three of us kept talking about it and talking about it, and I kept trying to use my connections to get something going with it. I was in South Africa doing a mini-series and George and Peter were in Toronto doing LAND, so we kind of put it away and we didn't do anything with it. One of their producers on LAND introduced them to a small company called Artfire, which was trying to get into the independent film business. Art Spiegel, who runs the company, and his partner Dan Fireman, who is part of the Reebok fortune, had this small company and they wanted to invest. Apparently, they were introduced to George...and DIARY came up.

Peter, very tenaciously, put together a terrific deal - you know I gotta hand it to Peter; he organized a really fantastic way of doing this movie. It was low budget, so we said yeah let's do it. We went to Toronto, where George lives now, and we made it in 23 days...and there it is!

I was lucky enough to be on set the night they filmed Greg Nicotero's cameo. I was wearing a Steelers hat and we talked about Pittsburgh...

Oh right! Yeah man, now I remember (laughs)! You saw what it was like. We were huffin'!

How did it feel to be working with George again?

It was kind of like going back to the old days, you know. George, Peter, and I would spend hours in his apartment talking about it. We wrote back and forth every day, which I'm not saying we made the film up as we went, because George sure had it in his mind. I gotta hand it to him, he really copped to that style and got it and did it. I really had to admire him because it was unusual for him, in terms of not only the shooting schedule, which was really tight, but the kind of hand held, all POV kind of film making. He did it better than any of the ones that have been out, as far as I'm concerned. I don't want to trash other movies, if you know what I'm talking about.

But it was great man. We're friends and we had a lot of laughs. It was a good collaboration again. We can talk openly about "well, why don't we try this...why don't we try that". As always, he came with a very clear vision of what he wanted to do, but he was open to "well how do we solve this problem" kind of stuff. It was just great fun.

George has no qualms admitting that he is slow to embrace technology, yet this film is shot in a way that he has never tried before and deals with the subject of the internet. It also has a cast of young people. What do you think made George tackle these topics now?

Well first of all, he wanted to do it because he wanted to go back to the kind of roots film making that he had when we were all in Pittsburgh, which was get a bunch of kids together and just do it. He was a kid then too, more or less. He's got a daughter who's in college at NYU now. I've got a son that's in college. So all of that stuff seeps in. I helped him with some of that, in terms of taking care of stuff on the computer when they're editing in the warehouse, stuff like that. I don't think that George is ever going to be a computer whiz, but he certainly understands the influence of it and the cultural impact of all of it. You would have to be living in a cave not to.

The interesting thing is it started off very much as a kid with a camera running around just documenting what was going on.

The more we talked about it, it evolved. For example, we talked about, well if we only have one camera, what are doing? Is it all single takes? How do we edit? How do we cut? So, we decided they have to get another camera. So, they find one in the hospital and they start using that. But we've been editing all along, how is that happening? Well then, we introduce the notion that what's been happening is Jason has been cutting it on his computer the whole time, unbeknownst to anybody. Alright, so why? Well, he's putting it on the internet. So all of that stuff just kind of evolved, it just happened. There was a practical reason for it as well as a commentary reason. It allowed us to have multiple cameras...all the normal film making stuff!

What about re-shoots or additional shooting? I read somewhere that the introduction of the Amish farmer was a re-shoot.

Well it wasn't a re-shoot, no. That's a misnomer. It was additional shooting. There were scenes that we had always thought about. What we did was we wrapped the film and said do we need them or not? The only way to know was really to cut the film and see how it was playing. After looking at a rough cut we decided, yeah you know it probably would be a good idea to have this. So we went back and we shot those scenes for a couple of days. But they were always scenes that George had in mind.

The marketing strategy by the Weinstein Company has been heavily criticized by the fans online. It opened in only a limited number of cities and there was no TV. advertising. Do you know why they decided to go the route they did?

No I don't, because I was not in Toronto when it was sold. Peter (Grunwald) explained it to me, but I don't really know. What Harvey (Weinstein) said, and I can only take him at his word, is that he has always wanted to find a horror film that he could treat like the art house movies when he and Bob (Weinstein) first started the company. Sort of platform it, build it slowly, play it out. But you need a certain kind of movie to do that. You don't do that with Saw or Hostel. He thought Diary had the right kind of stuff, whatever you want to

call it, that warranted treating it like that. Make it a hard ticket, something that people really had to see and had to go out of their way to see. I think also he felt that trying to open it wide in 2000 theaters, against whatever else was opening wide, and gave it a whole different kind of feel. Box office wise, it did well per screen. I don't know how much wider they are going to release it. That was the strategy, for right or wrong. Sometimes it works and sometimes it doesn't. I'm not saying that it hasn't worked. I think there are people who are frustrated, like my son for example. He goes to Lehigh University in Bethlehem, Pennsylvania. He can't find it unless he drives to Philly, so he's pissed! (Laughs)

How important was it to have Greg Nicotero on board? And was it difficult to get people like

Quentin Tarantino and Simon Pegg to do voice over work?

Well we wanted Greg involved in the project, first of all because he is great at what he does and also because the fans love his work. So that's a no brainer. He loves George and he's been a part of the "family" for a long time. As far as getting the other guys involved, it was just a matter of a phone call. They all wanted to do it right away.

Can you talk about your very own cameo?

(Laughs) Well that's kind of a running joke with me and George. He had a project once, called The Assassination, with Ed Harris. Richard Nixon plays a role in it and he wanted me to play Nixon. He thinks I'm always good for those types of government roles and corporate guys. So when the thing came up about doing FEMA, he said "well you're going to be the FEMA guy "(in the film, John's image is featured on a news broadcast as the head of FEMA)." That was second unit stuff. All that stuff that's on the TV, the stuff on the computer when Jason is editing it, and the phone with the Japanese woman, and all that other stuff. We needed to have that stuff pre-made so that it could play back on the day. In the first couple of days of film making, I went off and did all that while George was shooting. When it got to the point of we need the FEMA guy in the TV insert, well I was there. (Laughs) So I put a tie on and they took my picture, and that was that!

Are there definite plans for a sequel? If so, will you be involved?

There is talk of a sequel. I can't tell you more about it now, there's not a lot to tell, so it's a little premature. It would depend on when it is. George, Peter, and I have talked about it. They've asked me, and I would love to. Yeah man, if I have the time and it can work out, I would love to do it again. But I honestly can't give you anymore.

And finally, how do you feel about how the film turned out?

Oh, I love it. I love it. It's very clever. I was really proud to be involved with it. Like any film there are little things here and there, little winces maybe. But at the end of the day, it is the movie we set out to make and that George set out to make. I was just really happy to be a part of it. I think it has something to say. I think it really is of the times. I think it's got great humor. It's got a couple of really great kill gags thanks to Greg, George, and Peter, who had really terrific ideas. We were always like; we can't just do gun shots and head splatters forever. What are we gonna do that is clever and new, and that we have not done before? It was a real collaborative effort. George creates the environment where he encourages the best to come out of everybody. I was thrilled to be a part of it and I'm proud of the movie.

Note: Special thanks to Michael Felsher for helping this interview happen and of course to John Harrison for his time and graciousness.

PART FIVE

NIGHT
OF THE
LIVING DEAD
30TH ANNIVERSARY EDITION™

CHILDREN
OF THE
LIVING DEAD

VINCENT GUASTINI

SPECIAL MAKE-UP EFFECTS

PERSONAL REFLECTIONS

NIGHT OF THE LIVING DEAD 30™ (1998)
CHILDREN OF THE LIVING DEAD (2000)

Bill Hinzman scared the shit out of me as a kid when my mom took me to see the film NIGHT OF THE LIVING DEAD™ in the 60s, and all I am is sad he is no longer around. The one thing I will always remember about Bill Hinzman is his smile and his laugh. As well as his casual nature in the way he talked or told a story. He also had a sparkle in his eyes every time he talked about his wife or his family he spoke with pride about anything involving Heidi Hinzman his daughter, who he was always mentioning her and talking her up. I never saw a man love his family more then he loved them. Bill was the ultimate family man. As far as scaring people he loved it. His laugh would have a mischievous kid like cackle when he dressed up as number one zombie for conventions and how he would tell me with glee a story about scaring or posing with a pretty girl for a photo session.

He seemed to never get tired of his fans, and or wavier to make any of them feel they were taking up to much of his time when they asked him a question. At conventions Bill would put on white make-up and growl at the crowds of fans and always had a smile. He truly loved to be recognized for what he did in NIGHT OF THE LIVING DEAD™ nor ever got bored telling the story of how NIGHT OF THE LIVING DEAD™ became such a classic.

(Photo by Bob Michelucci)

For NIGHT 30 I was asked to recreate and make new Ghoul makeups using modern day prosthetics for the 30TH anniversary special edition release. I was very excited by this job at the time, I mean to recreate Bill into the famous cemetery ghoul, make him look the way he did 30 years ago. "It's like being asked to recreate Frankenstein, only thank god the actor is still alive! I also had to make a horde of new ghouls for new posse hunt scenes and eating scenes, which was added to the 1968 classic filmed with the original camera, and film stock. So was a blast to work on it even though were poorly received, I had a blast working with him and Russo and the whole Pittsburgh crowd. I loved Bill, the days walking around his farm and home cooked meals by his wife Bonnie will be very precious memories for me. I do still have Bill.

Karl Hardman and Marilyn Eastman ham it up with Vince on the set of NOLD30. (Photo by Bob Michelucci)

In one way he and his life mask cast hang on my wall in my studio so Bill is with me every day that I go to work. I also have a picture that was signed by him at the time I did his make-up and it says, "I'M COMING TO GET YOU Thanks Vince for raising me back from the Dead." At the time of his death I reread that and noticed how creepy it was in a way reading that. But then it dawned on me and I laughed to myself. Because I know Bill would laugh about that autograph on my wall because that's Bill, always laughing always trying to scare you, I miss you Bill, thanks for being a friend to me and sharing your love you had for movies, your fans, and your family.

HEIDI HINZMAN

ACTOR

PERSONAL REFLECTIONS

FLESHEATER (1988)
NIGHT OF THE LIVING DEAD 30™ (1998)
CHILDREN OF THE LIVING DEAD (2000)

Heidi is no stranger to zombies. Her whole life she was surrounded by zombies...one in particular stands out. That is her father, Bill Hinzman who is probably the most famous zombie of all time. He played the cemetery zombie in the original 1968 film NIGHT OF THE LIVING DEAD™.

Growing up, I always thought it was cool seeing my dad on TV. My dad, you see, was one of the most famous zombies ever. His name was Bill Hinzman and he was the cemetery zombie at the beginning of the classic NIGHT OF THE LIVING DEAD™. I remember that I would watch that movie and cheer him on! Making movies was just something that we did for fun, or at least that's what I thought as a young girl. As a little girl, I would sit under my father's camera tripod and watch them film movies such as dad's FLESHEATER all day. Dad was also a director and cinematographer. Acting in these films was just a lot of fun for me.

I began playing a zombie at a very young age. I think I was only seven or eight at the time. I played the little angel in FLESHEATER. I still have very vivid memories of this film. Too many to mention here, but the scene that I did with my father was amazing! "Aren't you supposed to say trick or treat?" I will never forget it.

Heidi answers the door in FLESHEATER (Photo courtesy Heidi Hinzman)

Getting "squibbed" and "shot" as a little kid was a little scary...but sooo exciting. I loved being able to sit in Jerry Gergley's make-up room and watching the effects come together. I also loved being made up as a zombie and getting to attack people. I remember everyone watching the barn burn was like having a party in the country. We all had blankets and lay in the grass while we watched it ablaze.

Years later, I accompanied my father to a horror convention and I couldn't believe that people actually were asking me for my autograph! It felt so strange. I never actually realized that people really had watched the films that we were making.

I was totally amazed back in 1993 at the Zombie Jamboree that was held in Pittsburgh to celebrate the twenty-fifth anniversary of the release of NIGHT OF THE LIVING DEAD™ that when the entire cast had reunited and walked the red carpet for a special screening of the film that so many people were lined up and screaming cheers to the cast. I remember that Kyra and I had such a blast riding in the limo to the event.

With dad on the set of FLESHEATER
(Photo courtesy Heidi Hinzman)

After dad passed away, the creator of the Spooky Empire con invited me and my niece to go to the Mayhem convention for a special celebration of my father's life and career. We were asked to lead the Zombie Walk that my father had led for them for years. It was really amazing to spend the weekend with so many fans who loved him so much. Over the years, dad had become friends with a lot of his fans and it was great to hear their stories of what a wonderful man he was. He was always so gracious with his fans. My father truly did love his fans. He loved getting dressed up and made up as his zombie character and heading to conventions all over the world. One of his proudest moments was leading a zombie walk in Spain where over two thousand people attended. NIGHT OF THE LIVING DEAD™ always put a smile on his face.

Being able to take part in the NIGHT OF THE LIVING DEAD™ 30th ANNIVERSARY EDITION was amazing. The idea was to add new additional footage to the original film so that the creators could regain copyright to the film. It was like getting the family back together again.

Heidi with her famous dad Bill Hinzman
(Photo courtesy Heidi Hinzman)

I was cast as Rosie from Beakmans Diner. Bob Michelucci designed the Beakmans Diner logo for my outfit. I spent three hours in the make-up chair, having to eat through a straw and having my arm painfully strapped behind my back every day. But I loved every minute of it. I will never forget filming that car crash with my NOLD family.

My next film playing a zombie, CHILDREN OF THE LIVING DEAD turned out to be a bit ridiculous. The

Heidi awaiting direction in between takes on the set of NIGHT OF THE LIVING DEAD 30 (Photo courtesy Heidi Hinzman)

As a zombie in CHILDREN OF THE LIVING DEAD
(Photo courtesy Heidi Hinzman)

original idea for the story by Jack Russo and my father had been reworked by the producer (and not for the better) but I still had the time of my life filming it. I made some great friends that I still get together with. BUT I HAD THE TIME OF MY LIFE FILMING IT in Los Angeles today. Again, I enjoyed being squibbed and shot and in this film I even got run over by a car and still kept going. It was also fun to come back to life as a zombie and rise out of a coffin. With this film, I was also a member of the crew, so I also had a chance to create some of the magic from the other side of the camera.

Today, I am fulfilling my dream by working in the film industry in Los Angeles.

Zombies never leave us

DEE MICHELUCCI

ACTOR

PERSONAL REFLECTIONS

NIGHT OF THE LIVING DEAD 30™ (1998)
"ZOMBIE MOM"

(Photo by Bob Michelucci) © *Image Ten, Inc.*

Being married to the author of this book, Bob Michelucci, for the past thirty-nine years has been very interesting and entertaining, if nothing else.

In 1977, a group of us were invited to Monroeville Mall to be made up and become zombie extras for George Romero's DAWN OF THE DEAD film. You see, Bob had become good friends with make-up and effects man Tom Savini around that time.

Bob was singled out to become one of the "special zombies that became affectionately known as the "Scope Zombie" in later years. The rest of us all went through the long line of zombies to receive the gray make-up treatment. As for my first experience at being a zombie, well unfortunately the scenes that I was in never made it to the final cut. Sigh.

All in all though, it was still a great and fun experience...especially when we all went across the street after the shoot and walked into an all-night pancake parlor still in our make-up! We received some really strange looks.

Our "Zombie" group for DAWN OF THE DEAD. Dee Michelucci is shown "Dead" center. (Photo courtesy Bob Michelucci)

It would take me more than twenty more years to get a second chance at zombie stardom. This time it would be in the special NIGHT OF THE LIVING DEAD™ 30th Anniversary Edition in 1998. My husband was working with John Russo and was one of the associate producers on the added footage part of the film. Guess what? They needed zombies! I was cast as the 'zombie mom" and our real-life daughter, Dawn, was cast as one of my "zombie daughters". Now there would be three zombies in our family.

As for my part, I became a zombie in the film after our car ran off the road and into a tree. All four of us were killed. My husband in the film, who was driving the car, was killed when he was impaled through the windshield with the tree trunk. As for the other three of us in the car, we rose again as zombies and as we slowly got out of the vehicle, we began to move around to the driver's side along with another horde of zombies approaching the accident scene to devour the driver!

(Photo by Bob Michelucci) © Image Ten, Inc..

I remember thinking to myself that my costume that consisted of a three quarter length coral pink dress, black dress shoes and a strand of white pearls around my neck reminded me of a "zombie" version of those famous mom's in the old TV programs such as *Leave It To Beaver, Dennis The Menace or Ozzie and Harriet!*

I was also in a couple of other scenes before finally being gunned down in a field along with other zombies by one of the posse members.

I had great fun and it gave me the opportunity to be in a classic horror film and work with some of the great classic original NIGHT OF THE LIVING DEAD™ celebrities like John Russo, Bill Hinzman and Russ Streiner.

(Photo by Bob Michelucci)   (© Image Ten, Inc.)

DAWN MICHELUCCI

ACTOR

PERSONAL REFLECTIONS

NIGHT OF THE LIVING DEAD 30™ (1998)
"ZOMBIE DAUGHTER"

(Photo by Bob Michelucci) © Image Ten, Inc..

As a 12 year old girl, in 1998, I had three dreams, all of which I got to fulfill because of my amazing opportunity to be in the 30th anniversary edition of the most well-known zombie flick, the one that I personally think was the start of the "zombie craze", NIGHT OF THE LIVING DEAD™.

My first dream as a young girl was to be a movie star! Well, I'm not sure if my small role can categorize me as a star, but I got to be in a movie! This opportunity was definitely one I will never forget. I remember being excited that I got to take a few days off from school... what can I say? I was a kid! But, what I remember most, was how much fun I had and how "cool" I thought it was to see how a movie was made, better yet, being a part of its creation.

I remember pulling up to the decrepit looking, kind of scary, house where the movie was being filmed. At the time we arrived it was still light out. Getting my make-up done was a ton of fun thanks to Vincent Guastini; and, seeing the transformation from me into a zombie was awesome! I do remember not being too fond of the fake blood in my hair though... it made some pretty big knots that were hard to get out!

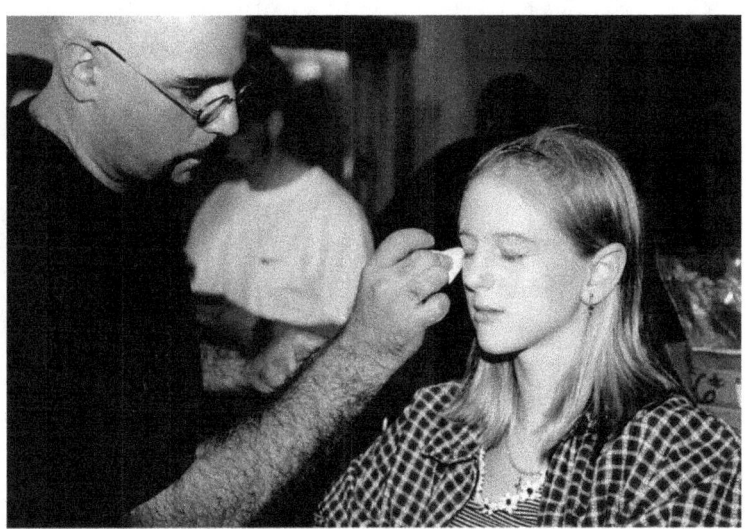

In make-up for NOLD30   (Photo by Bob Michelucci) © Image Ten, Inc..

Once that was all done, and it started to get dark out, the real fun began! I got to play car crash victim #1. The car was already wrecked into the tree when I arrived and my fake "dad", who was a mannequin with half his head chopped off by a tree limb, was already in the car. A quite funny fact that not everyone may know, is that my "dad's" brains that me and the other zombies got to eat, was actually ham barbeque from lunch earlier that day.

Doing the zombie walk in NOLD30 (© Image Ten, Inc.)
(Photo by Bob Michelucci)

Shoot after shoot I did the same thing... on "action" I very slowly opened my eyes first, and then slowly turned my head straight forward. It had been cocked to the left from the impact of the accident. And even more slowly, turned and got out of the car. Once I was out, I "zombie walked", kind of dragging my leg and limping slowly with my head cocked down, around the car and towards my "dad". I remember doing the scene quite a few times until me, car crash victim #2, and my "mom", who happened to be my real mom got it just right. This scene was actually one of the main scenes that were added to the movie.

I was also in two additional scenes; one where I was "slow-chasing" another zombie for a bite of an arm, and again in the cemetery scene where I was shot dead... well dead again. Ha-ha. The cemetery scene was pretty fun, learning how to fall the correct way at the correct time from being shot. I will say though, I was a little scared during the car crash scene because it was pitch black outside, the fog machines were rolling, and there were a ton of "zombies" coming up over the hill for the next scene! It definitely sent a chill through my body!

I remember being interviewed for the "extras" on the DVD and being asked if my parents named me Dawn because my dad played the "Scope Zombie" in the original DAWN OF THE DEAD. Well, though it *is* a crazy coincidence, I was not named after the film... my mommy just always wanted a Dawn Marie!

Let's get back to my three dreams at such a young age. The second was that I always wanted to go to Hollywood! Well, because I was in NOLD 30th, I got to go to Hollywood, CA with my parents to a horror convention to sign autographs! Being so young, I remember being kind of embarrassed and almost scared that no one would want my autograph. However, I did get to sign a few, and I must say... it felt good!

My third, and final dream at that age was to meet *N S Y N C. (Hey, I was 12!). Well, a big thanks to my daddy, Bob Michelucci and Vincent Guastini... my final dream came true! At the time, Vinnie worked for

Saturday Night Live and one day after school my dad surprised me and told me that we were going to New York to meet * N S Y N C! Vinnie got us back stage and sure enough I got to meet them, got a few hugs and autographs, and even a picture or two. I even met Joshua Jackson, who was the host that night, as well as Britney Spears, who just happened to be there with Justin Timberlake before anyone even knew that they were dating!

All in all, I have to say that my experience with NIGHT OF THE LIVING DEAD™ 30th was an amazing one. Although I didn't have any lines that I had to remember, I got to learn how to zombie walk, fall from getting shot properly, how to take direction, and the process of how a movie was made. I feel extremely blessed to have had that experience of a lifetime in such a well-known and classic movie, no less *and* to have the only three dreams I had at that time actually come true! Not too many people can say that at that age, if ever! I am truly grateful! I even made it into the newspaper and got to see myself on TV on Cinemax too!

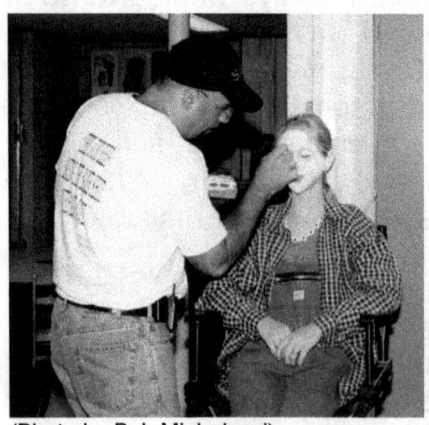

(Photo by Bob Michelucci)

DEBBIE ROCHON

ACTOR

PERSONAL REFLECTIONS

NIGHT OF THE LIVING DEAD 30™ (1998)

© Image Ten, Inc..

Debbie Rochon was a child of the streets and victim of much abuse growing up in British Columbia, Canada until she accidentally ended up in a featured extra role in Paramount's LADIES AND GENTLEMEN, THE FABULOUS STAINS (1982)!

That event changed her life. She saved enough money to move to New York City and study acting at age 17. After many years working with numerous theater companies in off-Broadway plays, she started to land small roles in films. (1990). Soon the parts grew bigger and bigger and primarily fell in the horror flick genre.

Debbie is the reigning Scream Queen and has starred in dozens of horror movies and has gained cult stardom worldwide.

When I heard that John Russo and Bob Michelucci, along with the rest of the Image Ten productions group formed in the 60s, were adding footage to one of my all-time favorite movies NIGHT OF THE LIVING DEAD™, I called them up. I didn't so much ask them if I could be in it - but kinda told them. OK, I insisted actually. There was a professional newscaster who was going to play the part I ended up with but because they had been such great friends over the years they gave the role to me.

I was extremely excited to be a part of the new footage that was being added because we were going to be shooting at some original NOTLD locations. Add to that the opportunity to work with such "Zombie Royalty" as Bill Hinzman, Marilyn Eastman, Karl Hardman, Russ Streiner et al. It was really this actor's dream. Although I had already seen the movie more times than I could count, I watched it numerous times before we shot so I could try and get the acting style of the time down best I could.

In 1988, I shot a movie with Duane Jones that was never released so this seemed like a very cool way of finally having the chance to 'share' the screen with him, even if it meant my scenes were being cut into a feature he had been shot 30 years prior.

The mood on the set was ecstatic. There wasn't a person there who wasn't thrilled to have the opportunity to be involved - and I was at the top of that list. The weather was in our favor for all of the outdoor scenes and the atmosphere on set was nothing short of magical. Regardless of how people feel about the NOLD30 project, I wouldn't have traded the experience for anything! It was also my first zombie film. Now that was a hell of an introduction working with the group of people who put the genre on the map!

Debbie in a scene from NOLD30 with Vlad Licina
(Photo courtesy Debbie Rochon)   © Image Ten, Inc.

Since my experiences on Night 30, I have done a number of zombie flicks. SKIN CRAWL a revenge-thriller that was shot in upstate New York, SICK BOY made by Tim and Sean Cunningham was shot in Texas, SOLID STATE a film directed by Stefano Milla shot in Italy and SICK directed by Ryan Andrews in Toronto were all great indie flesh features. The most recent "undead" film that I've made is called VIKINGS Vs. ZOMBIES which was shot in CT. and composed entirely against a green screen.

I am very happy that zombie films continue to entertain. There is nothing more fun that getting to act with flesh-eaters - and even more fun playing one! This is by far one of my favorite genres to work in.

(Photos courtesy Bob Michelucci)